Aristotle the Philosopher

J. L. Ackrill

Aristotle the Philosopher

Oxford New York Toronto Melbourne

OXFORD UNIVERSITY PRESS

1981

Oxford University Press, Walton Street, Oxford OX2 6DP

London Glasgow New York Toronto
Delhi Bombay Calcutta Madras Karachi
Kuala Lumpur Singapore Hong Kong Tokyo
Nairobi Dar es Salaam Cape Town
Melbourne Wellington

and associate companies in
Beirut Berlin Ibadan Mexico City

First published 1981 as an Oxford University Press paperback
and simultaneously in a hardback edition

British Library Cataloguing in Publication Data

Ackrill, J. L.
Aristotle the philosopher.
1. Aristotle – Philosophy
I. Title
185   B485
ISBN 0-19-219131-4
ISBN 0-19-289118-9 Pbk

Printed in Great Britain by
Richard Clay (The Chaucer Press) Ltd
Bungay, Suffolk

Preface

My aim in this book is not just to impart information, but to arouse interest in the philosophical problems Aristotle tackles, and in his arguments and ideas. I have tried to bring out the extraordinary range and the excitement of his philosophical investigations, and to show why he is so highly regarded by contemporary philosophers. I very much hope that readers of the book will want to go on to read Aristotle for themselves.

A fuller account of the aims and contents of this book will be found in Chapter 1.

I am most grateful to Henry Hardy and Judith Ackrill for their encouragement and advice, and to Elsie Hinkes for her skilful typing.

Oxford, September 1980   J. L. A.

Contents

1 Introduction

The aim of this book

This book is a guide-book to Aristotle's philosophy. I want, in this chapter, to make clear what *sort* of guide-book I have written, and also to say something about the territory it explores.

It might be thought that a guide to Aristotle the philosopher could just give an account of his doctrines. What they are must by now be well known to experts, and all that is needed is to summarise them as clearly as possible for non-experts. Far from it. Contrary to some traditional assumptions, Aristotle's philosophy is in various ways 'open', and not a closed set of doctrines. Why *is* Aristotle always credited with 'doctrines' – when other philosophers are said to have views or to make suggestions or to advance theories? There are, I think, two reasons. First, he does aim at developing a systematic and comprehensive philosophy, and at reaching final and correct conclusions about the questions examined. He often relies on conclusions from one enquiry when conducting another, and he often propounds his conclusions with confidence. In short, he seems to have the key to a vast range of problems, and to speak with great authority. Secondly, his works were studied for a long time as if they really did contain a set of authoritative doctrines. His 'treatises' or 'teachings' were regarded as the last word. Students were not encouraged to appraise them critically, but simply to learn and accept the truths they undoubtedly contained.

In fact, an account of Aristotle's philosophy as a set of doctrines must be terribly misleading. For his work extended over many years, from his student days in Plato's Academy to his death at the age of sixty-three. During this time his ideas developed and sometimes changed, he dropped old arguments and invented new ones, he handled central themes in a variety of contexts and with a variety of weapons. It follows that any serious understanding of his thought must allow for its *movement*, and not treat it as a mere catalogue of conclusions. Moreover, Aristotle's whole approach to philosophy is open and argumentative, and not dogmatic: he claims to proceed – and to a large extent he does proceed – by raising questions, laying out problems, and trying out possible answers or strategies. I must not exaggerate here. It is true that

Aristotle often adopts a headmaster's style, and speaks with assurance as if on the matter in hand final truth has been achieved; and certainly he has an *ideal* of final and comprehensive philosophical understanding of the world. Nevertheless, through most of his work there also rings, more or less loudly, the note of caution and of questioning: much remains obscure or uncertain, the answers to one set of problems throw up new ones, on important issues arguments may seem evenly balanced. An account of Aristotle's philosophy as a set of doctrines would take all the life and liveliness out of it. It is more like a developing series of problems with a developing series of responses.

What really characterises Aristotle as a philosopher is not the number and weight of his conclusions (his 'doctrines'), but the number and power and subtlety of his arguments and ideas and analyses. It is as well that this should be so. For having to learn a doctrine is a boring task, and specially depressing if you know that it is false; but interesting arguments give pleasure and profit whether or not they really establish the alleged conclusions. Modern astronomers decisively reject Aristotle's account of the heavenly bodies, but it remains of the greatest interest to see what *arguments* led him to conclude that the universe must be an eternally moving sphere. Again, Aristotle's key ideas have provoked and stimulated philosophers over many centuries – precisely because they are *not* cut and dried doctrines, but can be applied and interpreted and developed in various ways.

It is, then, a popular misconception to think of Aristotle as the great 'knower' who has wrapped up all the problems and mysteries of philosophy in neatly packaged and clearly addressed parcels. (The misconception derives from the attitudes and beliefs of some 'Aristotelians' in antiquity and the middle ages.) My next point may be rather more controversial. It seems to me both enjoyable and rewarding to engage in philosophical argument *with* Aristotle. Just as a tyro flautist enjoys the technique and performance of a master, so we enjoy the refinement, conciseness and suggestiveness of Aristotle's arguments – and we enjoy them the more, the more we engage ourselves in them. Now if our aim is *only* to *understand* Aristotle, this 'engagement' will have to be carefully limited; we must enter into his thoughts but not go beyond them, we must try to relive his intellectual journey, taking care not to carry with us any twentieth-century baggage or equipment. To achieve such an understanding is certainly a worthwhile aim, calling for both imagination and intellectual power. However, we may desire not only to gain some understanding of Aristotle, but also to understand better some of the philosophical problems he confronts. In this case we are entitled to engage him in argument as if he were a contemporary. He has an enviable ability to put a problem or an answer in a nutshell, and his crisp sentences are infinitely thought-provoking. If one of his sentences or arguments provokes us to questioning of our own or to counter-argument, we need not feel guilty because we are approaching an ancient philosopher with modern weapons. Aristotle himself will not mind; we can be sure that if he is in the Isles of the Blessed he is arguing away, using all the intellectual tools that are available to him. Certainly we shall have a less pure historical understanding of Aristotle, if our minds let in twentieth-century thoughts and concepts. But why should we not make that sacrifice if we wish? It is not in itself a fault to use modern notions in discussing arguments in ancient philosophers, and to argue with them as if they were contemporaries. It is a fault (the fault of anachronism) only if one's aim and claim is to be doing purely historical work.

To argue with Aristotle, and to learn from him, is not difficult. For the problems he struggled so hard to formulate are still central to philosophy, and the concepts and terminology he used in trying to solve them have not lost their power. My aim in this book is to rouse active interest in his philosophy as well as to convey information about it. So I have raised philosophical questions and made philosophical comments of my own, in order to remind the reader that what Aristotle says is there to be argued about, and to provoke him into further thought on the various problems.

Aristotle's works are arranged in a systematic way: first come logical treatises, then a long series of works on nature (themselves ordered according to a rational plan), then the metaphysical books, and finally works on 'practical' subjects – ethics, politics, rhetoric, aesthetics. These texts were edited and put into this order after Aristotle's death. He did not himself write them in that order, and it would give quite a wrong impression to expound his philosophy as if he had done so. In fact it is rather misleading to imply that he wrote them, as we have them, in any order at all. For although some are in a finished form and a polished style, many still bear the marks of the lecture-room; they are more like a lecturer's notes than the final draft of a book for publication. Since Aristotle gave lectures over many years, and returned to the same problems time and again, he naturally made corrections and additions to his notes. When his editor came to publish them to the world, he did not wish to risk losing anything important. He did not cut out superseded passages or eliminate alternative versions, but incorporated them into the text to be published. So a treatise, as we have it, is liable to contain earlier and later strata; there are often repetitions and sometimes inconsistencies. In some cases, notably the *Metaphysics*, a number of originally different courses were brought together into the form of a single work with a single title. Where necessary the editor would add a sentence here or there to gloss over an awkward transition, and so to strengthen the appearance of unity and continuity throughout the whole corpus of work.

Aristotle's philosophy is not a single, rigid system; nor can the treatises be set out and expounded in a simple chronological order. The real unity in his work is to be found in method, style and intellectual character, and in the pervasiveness of some key ideas and of some terminology. I shall try to bring out this unity. By quotation I shall hope to give a direct impression of Aristotle's manner of philosophising. (In making the translations I have aimed at reasonable accuracy rather than at smoothness or elegance; my comments and additions are enclosed in square brackets.) As to the ground covered, and the order of treatment, I have tried to write chapters any of which can be read on its own, but which together will give the reader a fair acquaintance with Aristotle's main ideas and a lively sense of his philosophical achievements. There is, of course, no question of being comprehensive – many major themes are not touched on at all; but at the end of the book I have offered advice on further reading.

Aristotle's life

It may be useful to give here a bare summary of the facts about Aristotle's life. He was born, the son of a doctor, at Stagira in Chalcidice (northern Greece) in 384 BC. At the age of eighteen he entered Plato's Academy at Athens, and he continued as a member for twenty years, until Plato's death in 347. The interrelation between these two philosophical giants, the young and the old, is a fascinating subject for study and speculation. It is clear that Aristotle was much influenced by Plato and by dialectical discussions conducted in the Academy, but he was also developing criticisms of Platonic theories and working on ideas of his own.

On Plato's death Aristotle left Athens and went first to Assos (on the coast of Asia Minor) and then to the island of Lesbos. Much of his empirical research into marine biology was done in this area. About 342 he was invited to go to Macedonia to supervise the education of the king's son, Alexander; unfortunately we know very little about how this project turned out. After a few years Aristotle returned to Athens and founded a new school (the Lyceum or Peripatos), in which research of all kinds – scientific, scholarly, philosophical – was conducted. The school flourished, but Aristotle himself left Athens in 323 for political reasons. He moved to Euboea, where he died a year later.

For more information about Aristotle's life and an account of the way in which his manuscripts were preserved, edited and transmitted to us, I can refer the reader to the books mentioned in the guide to Further

Reading, under the heading 'General', on page 156. They also say something about the chronology of his works and about the relation between his philosophy and Platonism.

Aristotle's philosophy

Greek philosophy begins with childishly simple questions and ends with complex and subtle theories. The questions which children ask are indeed liable to open up large difficulties and baffling problems. Where does the flame go when the candle is blown out? Where do I go when I die? How fast does time pass – and what is time? Who made God? Conscientious parents try to give some kind of answer to their children, but they do not themselves feel much exercised by such odd questions. Philosophers do; and as they try to make clear what is involved in them, and how such problems are to be solved (or shown to be unreal), they find themselves studying the very basis of our thought about the world and talking about the general nature of reality. They are led to develop and discuss ideas of great abstractness, and eventually to grapple with questions that look highly technical and very far removed from the child's original wonder.

Where *does* the flame go? Well, it just disappears; it is not a *thing*, and it does not *go* anywhere. What then is a *thing*? What disqualifies flames from being things? A flame, after all, is not an illusion or a mere appearance: appearances don't burn pieces of paper. Is it that things have to be made of some material? But surely a flame is made of something, even if the layman cannot say exactly what? Anyone who persists in trying to answer the flame-question is forced to examine a number of difficult questions about things and characteristics, about matter and change and identity. These are basic notions which we all use and rely on, but it proves very hard to analyse and understand them.

Where *do* I go when I die? Do I, like a flame, just vanish; or do I survive in some shape or form? The question is not one that calls just for religious faith or for scepticism. Before we can take a position about the *truth* of the claim that a person survives death we need a clearer understanding of the claim itself. What sort of a thing is an 'I'? Does it make sense to suggest that a soul, having been the soul of a living person, might go on existing after that person's death – after the body has stopped functioning? If 'I', or my soul, *can* exist disembodied, can it also enter into bodies other than mine? (Can there be soul-transplants as well as heart-transplants?) Does it make sense to say 'I used to be Napoleon', or 'Napoleon and I are really the same person'? Questions about mind and body, and about personal identity, are among the philosopher's most intriguing and difficult problems.

The child, about to be punished for some misdeed, claims that he couldn't help it. 'Of course you could,' we reply, as we administer the penalty. But how could we deal with his claim if we allowed ourselves to take it seriously? We should find ourselves having to explain, and if possible justify, the grounds on which we hold people responsible for some things but not for others. Any such explanation will lead quickly into puzzles about free will and determinism. If a person acts – as surely he does – in accordance with his beliefs and desires, and if one cannot *choose* what one believes or desires, how can anyone *ever* help doing what he does? He necessarily does what seems best to him at the moment – and he is no more *responsible* for what seems best to him than he is responsible for how the music sounds to him. Great practical issues, as well as complicated theoretical ones, are at stake here.

Small children are sometimes devoted to imaginary friends and chatter happily to invisible companions. It is natural to say that these friends and companions do not exist. 'But when I am thinking about my friend, I am not thinking about *nothing*. And when I am talking to my friend I am not talking to *nothing*. *Something* is being thought about or talked to – and if not my friend, then who or what is it?' Some such nursery paradox is at the heart of Parmenides' thought. Parmenides (born about 515 BC), the most sensational of the earlier Greek philosophers, argued and tried to prove that *what is not* cannot be said or thought: the very idea that *What is not, is* involves sheer contradiction. So whatever *can* be thought or said must *be*. It follows from this that plurality is impossible, since to say that there are two things is to imply that one of them is not the other. It also follows that change and movement are impossible, since these involve the idea that something is or becomes what it *was not*, that it *is not* what it was. Parmenides' remarkable poem – for he wrote his abstract logical arguments in hexameter verse – powerfully influenced both Plato and all subsequent Greek philosophy. In one direction it led towards an other-worldly metaphysics: reality is eternally unchanging, and one; this world of many changing things is appearance only. In another direction it led to much logical progress: to see through the Parmenidean paradoxes required fundamental enquiries into the nature of thought, of meaning and of truth. Plato took the first giant steps in his dialogue the *Sophist*; the journey to complete understanding of these matters is not yet over.

Aristotle is close enough to the beginning of philosophy to enable him still to feel and formulate simple questions without embarrassment, and to see clearly in outline the general shape of possible answers. He is not burdened, as we are, with a vast inheritance of technical terms and theories. On the other hand he is advanced enough, and clever enough, to argue with sophistication, and to develop ideas and theories that are subtle and fertile. This blend of almost childish directness with intense intellectual power is part of Aristotle's peculiar piquancy. It is what makes him a philosopher so easy to approach and so difficult to leave.

Some topics and ideas

Because Aristotle's work ranged over so many areas of philosophy, and laid the foundations of most of them, his main themes and ideas have never been entirely out of fashion, although he has been more highly regarded in some periods than in others. The interests of contemporary philosophers are exceptionally close to Aristotle's. Many of our most eagerly discussed problems are problems he raised, and many of our most characteristic philosophical moves are moves he invented or powerfully exploited. Many of his achievements are better understood and appreciated now than ever before. In this section I will give a small assortment of examples to illustrate these points; some of the topics mentioned will of course come up for fuller examination later.

Formal logic   Aristotle's famous – or notorious – theory of the syllogism (see Chapter 6) has often in the past been criticised and laughed at for being pedantic and arid, and for being quite untrue to the facts of human reasoning. But since the development of a rigorous mathematical logic we have come to see that the theory was in fact an extraordinary achievement in formal logic. Starting more or less from scratch Aristotle produced an almost perfect and impressively rigorous piece of logic – which can be properly valued only at a time when the ideals of completeness and rigour in logic are themselves understood and accepted.

Philosophy of mind   The mind–body problem (see Chapter 5) is a perennial. Traditionally seen as the problem of how two fundamentally different kinds of thing can interact (or how two totally different sets of events can be interrelated), it has recently been tackled in refreshingly new ways. The two main views advanced in contemporary discussion are (i) that mental events just *are* physical events of a special sort (identity theory); and (ii) that psychology does not deal with a special sort of thing or event at all, but rather with a special set of concepts, concepts which we use to describe and interpret physical and physiological events in a certain way, explaining them by reference to the functioning and survival of the animal (functionalism). Aristotle too decisively rejects dualist theories of the mind and body. Whether his own account can safely be described, as by a recent writer, as a 'sophisticated functionalism' is open to argument; but it certainly has strong pre-echoes of this theory, and also of identity theory. Aristotle's mastery of biology, and his interest in all forms of life, prevented him from being obsessed with difficulties about private mental experiences and self-consciousness, and led him to concentrate on an analysis of the various living functions, and of their interrelations, and on an account of their physical basis. This is also the drift of recent philosophy of mind.

Metaphysics This subject survived the attack of logical positivists in the 1930s and 1940s, and has been flourishing lately – under new management. Recent work recognises the key role of language in determining and expressing our conceptual scheme, and concentrates on descriptive rather than revisionary metaphysics – to use a contrast formulated at the beginning of one of the most influential books published in this field since the Second World War, P. F. Strawson's *Individuals* (1959). The topics of very many books and articles published since then (not least in the United States) are straight out of Aristotle. Things and qualities, matter and change, count-nouns and mass-words, subject and predicate: such topics are at the centre of Aristotle's investigations. And his approach to them has the same linguistic emphasis and sensitivity as that of recent metaphysicians. Some of his enquiries once seemed rather technical and uninspiring, compared with bolder flights of imaginative creativity; but we can now recognise them as first-class and still fascinating efforts, not to open up a new world, but to illuminate this one and to enhance our understanding of it.

Ethics Contemporary work on ethics has many Aristotelian features and roots. Distinguished modern philosophers have renewed discussion of questions raised by Aristotle – and have recognised their debt to him. I will pick out just two examples, both concerned with human action. J. L. Austin's paper 'A Plea for Excuses', first published in 1956, has provoked subtle and important work on responsibility, and on the various ways in which an agent may disclaim responsibility or seek to excuse or justify his action. The topic and the basic approach – through careful study of excuse-phrases like 'by accident', 'in ignorance', 'involuntarily', 'under duress' – come directly from book III of Aristotle's *Nicomachean Ethics*, a text that Austin himself had studied and discussed with pupils and in classes over many years. My second example is the American philosopher Donald Davidson. In a series of influential papers (republished in *Essays on Actions and Events*, 1980) he has examined the distinction between actions and events, the connection between the causes and the reasons for action, and the nature of *akrasia* (acting against one's own best judgement). All of these are central Aristotelian topics, and some of Davidson's answers are Aristotelian answers. Here as elsewhere Aristotle's remarks are crisp and condensed, sometimes to the point of obscurity. But because they contain the thought of a philosophical super-genius they repay repeated study and reflection.

Philosophy of science In his work on scientific explanation Aristotle's main interests include problems that are alive and kicking today. There is still debate on the nature of scientific explanation and the structure of scientific theories. Problems about teleology are still urgent in the biological sciences: what is the justification for explaining processes by reference to their ends or goals, and how are such explanations related to explanations given in terms of the ordinary natural laws that govern all physical processes? Finally, problems about natural necessity and essential definition are flourishing again, although they were once thought dead. Definitions in science are not, after all, just verbal abbreviations. They often encapsulate important discoveries, and they may give the real nature or essence of a kind of thing (or event or phenomenon) not previously fully understood. Some of Aristotle's discussions about types of definition, and about the role of definitions in science, link up quite clearly with work by such recent writers as Hilary Putnam and Saul Kripke (see pp. 60–1 and 99–105).

Philosophical logic I will mention just a few points. (i) Interest in categories, and in categorial and type-differences, goes back to Aristotle. He examined such differences enthusiastically and often, and he made good use of them – as have modern philosophers – in solving or dissolving philosophical puzzles. The category arguments that dominate that twentieth-century classic, Gilbert Ryle's *Concept of Mind* (1949), were first hewn in Aristotle's workshop. (ii) Questions about identity and individuation have absorbed many philosophers lately; they are questions crucial for logic and metaphysics. Aristotle often addressed himself to them, and he made important steps towards answering them. Thus, for example, he recognised that 'Is it the same?' needs to be completed: 'Is it the same *so-and-so*?' It is only with respect to some classification or description that questions about sameness can properly be raised and answered. (iii) Powerful ideas in recent philosophy are those of sense and reference, and of referential opacity. The ideas, though not the labels, are familiar to Aristotle, and they are used by him in all sorts of contexts. We say that 'the morning star' and 'the evening star' have the same reference but a different sense. He would say that the morning star and the evening star are the same, but their being is not the same; being the morning star is not the same as being the evening star, although the morning star is in fact the same star as the evening star. As regards opacity, Aristotle's key phrases are 'in itself' and 'by accident' or 'incidentally' (*per accidens*). If *a* is *b* not in itself by only *per accidens*, you cannot substitute '*b*' for '*a*' in a true sentence and be sure that your new sentence will also be true.

2 Aristotle at work

In this chapter I want to mention some of the general characteristics of Aristotle's philosophising, and then to give a few examples by way of illustration.

Some features of Aristotle's philosophising

Aristotle usually begins any major enquiry with a survey of the views of his predecessors. Any such view, he thinks, is likely to contain some element of truth, and that we must try to preserve. The points where previous thinkers are in conflict with one another provide the problems we have to solve. A proper solution, a full understanding of the topic, should enable us to see not only who was right and who was wrong on a given issue, but also why the erroneous view was adopted.

Aristotle's attitude to his predecessors is that of a philosopher rather than a historian. He sees them as aids to reaching the truth; he is not seeking to give a full and accurate account of each of them for his own sake. His summaries of their views are often expressed, anachronistically, in his own terminology; he often reads back into them ideas and questions of his own.

Not only the views of previous thinkers, but also what ordinary people say, must form part of the material from which philosophical enquiries start. A good deal of Aristotle's work is concerned with conceptual clarification, with trying to understand and analyse ideas that are in a way already familiar. Ordinary language provides essential clues here, even if in the end some revision – some tidying up – of how we usually speak and think may prove desirable. Many of Aristotle's most characteristic and important ideas emerge from discussions of what people ordinarily say. The key terms of his philosophy are not highly technical; they are simple and ordinary words and phrases. Thus, for instance, in order to distinguish substance from other kinds of entity he uses 'What is it?' as a label, since it is by applying this ordinary question – as opposed to questions like 'Where is it?' or 'How big is it?' – that he first picks out the category of substance. Again, where he is examining – as we should put it – the relation between facts and their explanations, he regularly speaks of 'the *that*' and 'the *because*'.

Aristotle's close attention to ordinary language helps to make his philosophy accessible – he does not sail off on a cloud of unexplained technical terms and abstractions. It also helps to give his style its attractive grittiness.

In some areas of enquiry it is necessary to go out and collect a great deal of factual evidence before one can usefully construct theories. Aristotle recommends and practises the habit of researching as widely as possible before starting to classify, generalise and theorise. ('It is a capital mistake to theorise before one has data,' as Sherlock Holmes puts it.) He did, or caused to be done, much systematic research, notably in biology, but also in historical studies.

It is true that Aristotle sometimes seems to settle large questions of fact in a highly unscientific way – using 'proofs' provided by reasoning where a telescope or accurate observations would have been more useful. He is naturally at his best, from this point of view, in biological studies, where close and skilful observations were possible, and where the lack of precise measuring instruments was not fatal. This is why he could still be hailed by Darwin as a genius, whereas his work on matter, movement and the heavenly bodies, though of absorbing interest to philosophers, is not required reading for modern physicists or astronomers.

In working out his views on a philosophical problem Aristotle likes to start by assembling all the puzzles and difficulties, along with the main lines of argument on both sides of every question. As he goes on to clear things up, he continues to operate dialectically, that is, by trying out objections to what he has himself said, and by raising new questions. He often recognises that obscurities remain, that what has been said is perhaps true enough, but not yet clear. He has a keen eye for difficulties and an insatiable appetite for argument, and he is never disposed to rest on his oars.

Aristotle distinguishes very sharply between different sorts of enquiry. Some can aim at a high degree of precision and certainty, others for various reasons cannot. 'It is the mark of an educated man to look for precision just so far as the nature of the subject in question admits of it. It is as foolish to accept merely probable reasoning from a mathematician as it is to demand demonstrative proofs from a rhetorician.' Aristotle is always delighted if he can find a knock-down argument, an almost mathematical proof or disproof. But in many areas philosophical argument has a looser texture. It involves not only deductive inferences, but also appeals to what is likely and reasonable, the drawing of analogies, the exploiting of clues from language, and so on. The philosopher's stock-in-trade includes a rich variety of persuasive devices and techniques as well as more rigorous forms of argument.

Aristotle at work

In what follows I give half a dozen assorted examples of Aristotle at work. Short quotations obviously cannot do justice to the process of persistent analysis and argument that large philosophical problems call for. But I hope to convey an idea of some of the ways in which Aristotle tackles questions, and to give some impression of his style. I have put in a few comments, by way of elucidation; one or two of the actual topics will be discussed in later chapters.

A conceptual enquiry: what is weakness of character and how does it differ from wickedness?

My first sample comes from Aristotle's discussion of *akrasia* in the *Nicomachean Ethics*. The word *akrasia* is often translated by 'incontinence' or 'weakness of will'; in what follows I have used 'weakness of character' or simply 'weakness'. The *akratic* person is one who acts against his own best judgement; he does what he realises he ought not to do. Aristotle wants to understand how this is possible, and to get clear how such weakness differs from sheer wickedness. The passages I will quote (from *Nicomachean Ethics* VII.2) are a good example of one of his characteristic methods of argument, and they also convey some impression of his close style of writing. He first outlines the procedure he will adopt.

> As with other topics we must first set out how things appear to be, and then, after developing the problems [*aporiai*], go on to prove the truth, if possible, of all the common beliefs [*endoxa*] about the matters in question, or failing that, of the majority of them and the most authoritative. For if we can solve the problems while leaving common beliefs untouched, we shall have proved the case sufficiently.

Aristotle next lists seven 'common beliefs' about weakness of character and strength of character.

(i) It is thought that strength of character is good and praiseworthy, weakness bad and blameworthy; and that (ii) the strong man is the man who stands by his reasoning, the weak man departs from it. (iii) The weak man knows that he is behaving badly but does so because of passion; the strong man knows that his desires are bad and does not follow them, because of his reason. (iv) People think that a temperate man is strong and unyielding, and some think that every strong man is temperate, while others do not. (v) Some think the wicked to be weak and the weak wicked, without distinction; others say that they are different. (vi) Sometimes it is said that the wise man cannot be a weak man, sometimes that some wise and clever people are weak. (vii) People are called weak [not only about bodily pleasures, but] also about anger, honour, and gain.

These then are the things that are said.

Now come some questions and puzzles (*aporiai*) derived from or suggested by these common beliefs.

One may raise these questions: (*a*) What *kind* of correct supposition has a man who acts weakly? [Does he *know* that what he is doing is wrong, or does he only *think* that it is? If a man really and truly knows what is the best thing for him to do, isn't he bound to do it? If, however, the akratic man is doing something that he only thinks to be wrong, can he be much blamed for that? These questions show that more needs to be said about (iii) above.] If strength of character involves having strong and bad desires [that is, the desires which the man of strong character will resist], the temperate person will not be a man of strong character, nor will a man of strong character be temperate (since a temperate person does not *have* excessive or bad desires). But strength of character certainly must involve having strong and bad desires. For if a man's desires are *good*, the state of character that prevents him from following them will be bad – so that not all strength of character will be good; while if the desires are *weak* then (whether they are good or bad) there is nothing special or great in not following them [so we must correct (iv) above]. (*b*) Further, if strength of character makes a man stand by any and every opinion, it is bad – if, that is, it makes him stand by even a false opinion; and if weakness of character is apt to abandon any and every opinion, there will be a good kind of weakness [this is a paradox derived from (i) and (ii) above]. . . (*c*) There is an argument from which it follows that folly plus weakness is virtue. For owing to weakness a man does the opposite of what he thinks he should, but he may think what is good to be evil and something that he should not do: the consequence is that he will do what is good and not what is evil [another form of the paradox in (*b*) above]. (*d*) Further, one who acts from conviction in pursuing and choosing pleasures would seem to be better than one who does so as the result not of reasoning but of weakness. [A thoroughly wicked and dissolute man would thus be better than a man of good principles and intentions who acted badly from weakness.] For he is easier to cure, since he may be persuaded to change his mind. To the weak man may be applied the proverb, 'When water chokes, what is one to wash it down with?' If he had been convinced of the rightness of his conduct, he would have desisted when persuaded to change his mind; but as it is he acts in spite of being persuaded of something quite different. [This is another paradox arising from (ii) above.] (*e*) Further, if there can be weakness and strength of character about everything, who is 'a weak man' without qualification? After all, nobody has all the forms of weakness, but we do say that some people are 'weak' without qualification. [See (vii) above.]

Of such a kind are the problems that arise. Some points must be refuted and others left standing. To solve the problem is to discover the truth.

Aristotle proceeds to consider whether a weak man acts with or without knowledge, and with what objects weakness and strength of character are concerned. The first of these enquiries (VII.3) opens up large questions about human action and how desire and belief are involved in its causation. The second (VII.4–5) brings into play a useful – and highly Aristotelian – idea, that a word may be used in various but related senses, one sense or use being primary ('without qualification') and the others derivative and secondary. There follows, in VII.6–10, further discussion of the different types of weakness, and of the relation of weakness to wickedness.

A fundamental practical question: what is the best life for a man?

In Chapter 7 of *Nicomachean Ethics* I Aristotle addresses himself to the question 'What is *eudaimonia*?' '*Eudaimonia*' is often translated 'happiness', but the English word has misleading suggestions, and in what follows I shall simply transliterate the Greek noun and adjective (*eudaimonia* and *eudaimon*). Aristotle is really asking the question – basic for morality – 'What is the very best and most worthwhile life that a man could possibly lead?' In the following famous and influential passage he approaches this question by enquiring what powers and activities distinguish human beings from other living things. What is the job or characteristic work (*ergon*) of a man as such?

To say that the best thing is *eudaimonia* may well seem a platitude. What we want is a clear statement of *what eudaimonia is*. Perhaps we

can get this if we get hold of what a man *does*. For with a flautist or
sculptor or any craftsman – or anything that has a particular thing to
make or do – it is in what it does that its good (and its doing well)
seems to reside. And so it would seem to be with man too, if there is in
fact anything for him to do. A carpenter and a cobbler have particular
products and things to make or do; has a *man* not got any, is he by
nature a do-nothing? Or rather, just as an eye, a hand, a foot, and in
general each part, obviously has a particular thing to do, so would one
take it that a man also, apart from all these, has his particular thing to
do?

Well then, what might this be? Living seems to be shared even with
plants, and we are looking for what is peculiar to men. So the life of
nourishment and growth must be set aside. Next [moving up from
plants to animals] would come a life of perception, but this too is
evidently shared with horse, ox and every animal. What is left then is
an active life of the part of men that possesses reason.

Aristotle now moves from the question what a *man*, as such, does, to the
question what a *good* man does; and he identifies this with the question
'What is the *good life* for a man?'

What a man has to do, then, is to live actively in accordance with
reason (or not without reason). But what an *x* and a good *x* have to do
is the same in kind – e.g. a lyre-player and a good lyre-player, and so in
general in all cases, superiority in excellence being added to what he
has to do: what a lyre-player does is to play the lyre, what a good one
does is to play it well. A man's good, therefore, turns out to be active
living in accordance with excellence, or – if there are a number of
excellences – in accordance with the best and most perfect excellence.
Moreover, in a complete life. For one swallow does not make a
summer, nor does one day; and similarly a man is not made blessed
and *eudaimon* by one day or by a short period of time.

In the next chapter (I.8) Aristotle checks the conclusion reached in this
passage by seeing whether it fits the things people ordinarily say about
eudaimonia. He finds that it does. The rest of the *Ethics* investigates the
various types of human excellence (of character and of mind), with a view
to filling out the very rough outline account of human well-being which
the above argument has provided.

The ideas on which Aristotle's argument about *eudaimonia* relies are
that a man's long-term well-being consists in his living the life appropriate to human nature, and that to discover what this nature is we must ask
what powers and activities are distinctive of man. Both of these ideas are

important and valuable, even though their application raises grave problems both in theory and in practice. Something more will be said on this topic in Chapter 10.

A semi-mathematical argument about weight and movement

In the *De Caelo* Aristotle starts from some very simple and plausible assumptions about matter and movement, and builds up a series of quite sophisticated arguments to establish a certain account of the universe. The cosmology he arrives at has often been derided, though since it was widely accepted for many centuries it must have an interest for the historian of ideas and culture. It is his arguments, however, rather than his conclusions that claim our attention today: it is still instructive and enjoyable to analyse them and to tease out their various strands.

One of the first points Aristotle seeks to establish is that the world is a finite and not (as many had thought) an infinite body. Among his arguments against the possibility of an infinite body there is one concerned with weight. He argues that the weight of an infinite body could not be *finite*, but that to suppose it *infinite* leads to contradiction. For an infinitely heavy body would move a given distance infinitely faster than any finite body. But however short the time it took, there would be *some* definite ratio between that time and the time taken by a finite body – so that it would not after all have moved *infinitely* faster. (If the infinite body took *no* time it would not have moved at all, since to move is to be at one place at one time and at another place at another time.) The following passage will serve as a tiny example of the semi-mathematical type of argument that is common in Aristotle's discussions of such topics as movement, time, and space.

It is clear from what has been said that the weight of an infinite body could not be finite. It would therefore have to be infinite. So if that is impossible, the existence of an infinite body is itself impossible. And that it is indeed impossible for there to be an infinite weight can easily be seen.

(i) If a certain weight moves a certain distance in a certain time, a greater weight will move the same distance in a shorter time, and the proportion which the weights have to one another, the times too will have, inversely. Thus if the half weight covers the distance in a certain time, the whole weight (its double) will cover it in half the time. (ii) A finite weight will cover any finite distance in a certain finite time.

From these two premises it follows that if there is an infinite weight it *must* move (since it is as great as a finite weight and greater), but on the other hand it must *not* move. For weights must move in a time related inversely to the difference of weight, the greater weight in the shorter time, but there is *no* relation of the infinite to the finite: a shorter time bears a relation only to a *finite* longer time.

It is therefore impossible for there to be an infinite weight ... and impossible therefore for there to be a body of infinite weight. (*De Caelo* I.6.273b29).

A question about memory

What is it to remember someone or something? A standard account would say that it involves having a memory-image of the person or thing, an image which is like the original sense-impression, a sort of feeble copy of it; the original experience must have left some 'trace', and it is that trace that is reactivated later as a memory-image. Whatever the limitations and defects of such a story, it is accepted by many philosophers as at least part of the truth about one kind of memory or recollection. Where and how memory-traces are stored is of course a matter for science. Aristotle supposes it to be in the heart. Sense-perception, he thinks, is or involves a movement starting from the perceived object and passing through the blood to the heart, the central sense-organ. There the movement persists unnoticed, but under certain circumstances it gets reactivated later and appears as an image. For heart and blood we might like to substitute brain and nervous system. But the important question that now asks itself is this: what more is there to memory than having such revived images? For obviously not every case of my having an image which is in fact a 'descendant' of an earlier sense-impression is a case of my remembering that impression (or the object then perceived). Part of the answer to this question is provided by Aristotle in his discussion of a problem he propounds in his little treatise on memory (after he has given the above-mentioned account of the processes involved). His problem is this: how can the having of an image now be the recalling of a person or experience of long ago?

How is it possible, when it is the image that is present, and the thing itself is absent, to remember what is not present? It is clear that one must think of what comes about through sense-perception in the soul (or in the part of the body which contains the soul) as being like a sort of picture, and having this is, we say, memory. For the change that occurs stamps in, so to speak, a sort of imprint of the sense-image (like people who seal things with signet-rings) ...

But if this is the sort of thing that happens with memory, is it the present affection that one remembers, or is it the thing from which it was produced? If the former, it will follow that we remember nothing which is absent. If the latter, how is it that while perceiving the image we remember what we are not perceiving, the absent thing? And if it is like an imprint or drawing in us, why should the perception of this be the memory of something else, rather than of the image itself? For it is *this* that one contemplates in exercising one's memory, and it is this that one perceives. So how is one to remember what is not present? At that rate it should be equally possible to see and to hear what is not present! (*De Memoria* 1.450a25)

Aristotle now makes effective use of his important idea that one and the same thing can be described or seen in different ways. He suggests that what has to be added to the earlier story about memory is something about how the person having the image regards it, whether he himself takes it *as* (or, takes it to be) a copy, left by a trace, of the original object. Remembering is not to be thought of as a form of direct awareness of the past; but it involves a belief about the past generated by looking in a certain way at a present image. (Compare the situation of a person looking at a canvas with paint on it and saying 'That is the Duke of Wellington.')

But perhaps this *is* possible and actually happens. For the figure drawn on a panel is both a figure and a likeness. One and the same item is both – though its being the one is not the same as its being the other; and one can contemplate it either as a figure or as a likeness. In the same way one must suppose the image in us to be something in its own right and also to be *of* something else. In so far then as it is something in its own right, it is an object of contemplation, an image; but in so far as it is of something else, it is a sort of likeness and a reminder. Hence whenever the relevant change is activated, if the soul perceives the image as it is in its own right, it is as a thought or image that it appears to come before us. But if one contemplates the image as being of something else and (as in the case of the drawing) as a likeness, e.g. *of* Coriscus (when one has not just seen Coriscus), then (not only in the case of the drawing is the experience of contemplating it *thus* different from when one contemplates it simply as a drawn figure; but also) in the soul the one image occurs simply as a thought, the other – because, as in the case of the drawing, it is a likeness – is a reminder. (*De Memoria* 1.450b20)

The ideas so briefly touched on here play a large part in recent discussions of perceptions, thinking, and understanding. The idea of taking something in a certain way – or using something in a certain way – has great importance in the account of meaning given by Ludwig

Wittgenstein (1889–1951), one of the most profound and influential of twentieth-century philosophers. But Aristotle's solution to the problem about memory leaves a number of doubts and difficulties. I mention three. (i) His account of memory draws a contrast beween an original perception and the later image, which may or may not be taken to be 'of' the originally perceived object. In fact, however, perception itself cannot easily be regarded as an immediate form of knowledge. Taking a sense-impression to be 'of' a real present object is surely quite analogous to taking a memory-image to be 'of' a past object. Perception as well as memory calls for the interpretation of data, and involves assumptions and beliefs. (ii) An epistemological question: What *right* can I have to take this image to be a likeness of a past object? How could I possibly *justify* my claim that this image is like such and such a past experience, when there can in principle never be the possibility of checking this alleged likeness by direct comparison? Equally, of course, with sense-perception itself: How can I ever verify my supposition that when having a certain sense-impression I am seeing a real thing? Such doubts are not felt by Aristotle. (iii) How is it *possible* to take a present image to be the likeness of something in the past? We have introduced this idea in order to explain a puzzle, how having a present image can amount to remembering something in the past. But a precisely similar puzzle remains: How can I, having a present image, *think* of something in the past? If I am to take my image to be an image of my long dead grandfather, I must think of my grandfather. The problem how one recalls something past via a present image has been replaced by the problem how one thinks of something past (or otherwise absent) via a present image. So although it is quite right to insist that belief enters into the analysis of memory, bringing it in does not solve the particular problem Aristotle starts from, the problem – to put it generally – of how thought can go beyond or transcend the immediately given.

Tomorrow's sea-battle: a famous argument about determinism

One of Aristotle's most provoking stretches of argument is contained in Chapter 9 of his short logical work *De Interpretatione*. He develops a plausible argument to show that everything that will ever happen will happen *necessarily*, brings out the extraordinary and unacceptable implications of this conclusion, and finally offers a solution to the problem. The chapter continues to excite interest and controversy: what Aristotle says may not be entirely clear, but it is clear that he is raising very deep questions about truth, time, and necessity.

Aristotle begins by claiming that statements about particular future events ('future singulars') differ from other statements in that they may be neither true nor false: 'There was a sea-battle in the straits yesterday' must be either true or false (and its denial must be correspondingly false or true); but 'There will be a sea-battle in the straits tomorrow' is perhaps not (or not yet) either true or false. To support this, Aristotle works out what follows from the assumption that all future singulars *are* either true or false (do have a 'truth-value'). If my prediction of a sea-battle tomorrow is true, there *must* be a sea-battle tomorrow; and if it is false, there *can't* be a sea-battle tomorrow. So, if my prediction is either true or false, either there *must* be or there *can't* be a sea-battle tomorrow – and there's no room for chance or alternative possibilities, no room for 'There *may* be a sea-battle tomorrow.'

> For if every affirmation or negation is true or false it is necessary for everything either to be the case or not to be the case. For if one person says that something will be and another denies this same thing, it is clearly necessary for one of them to be saying what is true – *if* every affirmation is true or false; for both will not be the case together under such circumstances. ['There will be a sea-battle tomorrow' and 'There will not be a sea-battle tomorrow' cannot both be true, and cannot both be false. So if they have a truth-value at all, one of them must be true and the other false.] For if it is true to say that it is white or is not white, it is necessary for it to be white or not white; and if it is white or is not white, then it is true to say or deny this. If it is not the case it is false, if it is false it is not the case. So it is necessary for the affirmation or the negation to be true. It follows that nothing either is (or is happening) or will be or will not be *by chance*, or as chance has it, but everything of necessity and not as chance has it (since either he who says or he who denies is saying what is true). For otherwise it might equally well happen or not happen, since what is as chance has it is no more thus than not thus, nor will it be.
>
> Again, if it is white now it was true to say earlier that it would be white; so that it was always true to say of anything that has happened that it would be so. But if it was always true to say that it was so, or would be so, it *could not* not be so, or not be going to be so. But if something cannot not happen it is impossible for it not to happen; and if it is impossible for something not to happen it is necessary for it to happen. Everything that will be, therefore, happens necessarily. So nothing will come about as chance has it or by chance; for if by chance, not of necessity. (*De Interpretatione* 9.18a34).

In the next part of the chapter Aristotle brings out how absurd and paradoxical this conclusion is: if everything happens of necessity there is no point in deliberating about what to do, and no sense to any talk of alternative possibilities. Finally, in the passage quoted below, he offers a way out of the difficulty. Unfortunately this passage is very concise, and it is not clear whether he is returning to the idea that future singulars lack a truth-value, that some predictions are not yet either true or false, or whether he is making a logical point intended to undermine the argument in the passage quoted above – the point, namely, that one cannot move from 'Necessarily either *p* or not-*p*' to 'Either necessarily *p* or necessarily not-*p*.' Is Aristotle saying that 'There will be a sea-battle tomorrow' is not yet true and not yet false; or that it is already true or already false, but not necessarily true or necessarily false? The reader may like to decide how the puzzle about tomorrow's sea-battle really *ought* to be solved or dissolved.

What is, necessarily is, when it is; and what is not, necessarily is not, when it is not. But not everything that is, necessarily is; and not everything that is not, necessarily is not. For to say that everything that is, is of necessity, when it is, is not the same as saying unconditionally that it is of necessity. Similarly with what is not. And the same account holds for contradictories: everything necessarily is or is not, and will be or will not be; but one cannot divide and say that one or the other is necessary. I mean, for example: it is necessary for there to be or not to be a sea-battle tomorrow; but it is not necessary for a sea-battle to take place tomorrow, nor for one not to take place – though it is necessary for one to take place or not to take place. So, since statements are true according to how the actual things are, it is clear that wherever these are such as to allow of contraries as chance has it, the same necessarily holds for the contradictories also. This happens with things that are not always so or are not always not so. With these it is necessary for one or the other of the contradictories to be true or false – not, however, this one or that one, but as chance has it; or for one to be true *rather* than the other, yet not *already* true or false.

Clearly, then, it is not necessary that of every affirmation and opposite negation one should be true and the other false. For what holds for things that are does not hold for things that are not but may possibly be or not be; with these it is as we have said. (*De Interpretatione* 9.19a23).

There was no first change and there will be no last change

Three books of the *Physics* contain an impressive and complex argument leading to the conclusion that there must be a first cause of all change, a cause which is eternal and itself changeless. The following passages are concerned to establish one of the crucial premises of the argument, that change has always been going on and always will go on. Aristotle first argues, both from his definition of change and from what 'everyone would agree', that any change – including any supposed *first* change – presupposes the existence of things capable of changing.

> Let us begin first from what we have established previously: change, we said, is the actualisation of the changeable *qua* changeable. There must therefore already exist the things capable of being changed (in each of the various ways). Indeed, even apart from the definition of change, everyone would agree that what is changed must be something capable of being changed (in each of the various ways: what is altered must be something capable of being altered; what is moved must be something capable of being transferred in place). There must therefore be something capable of being burnt before there is the being burnt, and something capable of burning before there is the burning. (*Physics* VIII.1.251a8).

Aristotle next argues that to explain how such things – things capable of changing – came into being at a certain time, or alternatively why they started at a certain time to exercise their capacity to change, we must assume some other change – which will have to have been *before* the supposed first change.

> Now these things themselves must either (i) have come into being at some time, having previously not existed, or (ii) be eternal. If (i) each of the changeable things came into being, there must have been – before the change in question – another change which brought into being the thing able to be changed (or able to bring about change). But if (ii) they already existed from eternity without change – this suggestion seems unreasonable at first sight, but still more so upon further examination. For if while there are some things capable of being changed and others capable of effecting it, there is to be a time at which something first effects change and something is changed, and another time at which nothing does so but it is at rest, this thing that is at rest must have undergone change previously. For there must have been some cause of its being at rest, i.e. of its stopping short of actual change. Therefore before the supposed first change there must have been a previous change [to remove whatever had caused the potentially changing things to stop short of actual change]. (*Physics* VIII.1.251a16).

This argument against the possibility of there being a first change is based on a principle about causation, the principle that there must be some explanation why any given change occurs and that the explanation must refer to some previous event. Aristotle next develops an argument from the concept of time. He draws on a conclusion reached in *Physics* IV, where time was found to be essentially connected with change – it is what measures change. He claims that since it is absurd to suggest that time could start or end, it is absurd to suggest that change could do so; for time exists only as measuring change.

> Moreover how is there to be a before and an after unless there is time, or time unless there is change? So if time is 'the number of change' [that in respect of which change is measurable] or is a kind of change, then, if there has always been time, there must always have been change also ... Now if it is impossible for time either to be or to be thought of without the 'now', and the now is a kind of intermediate, combining both a beginning and an end (a beginning of time to come and an end of time past), there must always have been time. For the extremity of any period of time taken to be the first or last will be in some 'now' (since in time there is nothing to get hold of *except* a 'now'), so that, since the 'now' is both a beginning and an end, there must on both sides of it always be time. But if time, evidently there must be change too, inasmuch as time is an aspect or attribute of change. (*Physics* VIII.1.251b10)

The rest of the chapter contains arguments against the possibility of a *last* change, and concludes that 'there was no time and there will be no time when there was not or will not be change'. Chapter 2 states and deals with some objections to this conclusion (including the interesting objection that in free human action we do *seem* to see something done, a change originated, *without* its being caused by a preceding change). By Chapter 6 Aristotle is ready to make the further large claim that the necessary eternity of change implies the existence of a single primary cause of change, an eternal 'unmoved mover', which he calls 'god'. On this see Chapter 9 below.

3 The analysis of change: matter and form

In this chapter and the next I want to expound, with the aid of quotation and paraphrase, a continuous chunk of text which develops ideas basic to much of Aristotle's philosophy and will provide a good starting-point for discussion of many problems. The chunk in question, *Physics* I–II, is about fundamental ideas of what we should call natural science (the word *physis* means 'nature'); so we might say that it is philosophy of science. But the ideas in question are so fundamental to our way of looking at the world that the books may equally well be regarded as metaphysics – indeed they are a paradigm of 'descriptive metaphysics'.

Aristotle begins the first chapter of *Physics* I by laying it down that to acquire knowledge or understanding of nature (or of anything else) it is principles, causes or elements that we need to grasp. The nuances of these words are in Greek as in English different; and we shall find that investigation reveals several different types of explanatory concept. (A full understanding of nature will involve knowing the answers to such diverse questions as: What is a leaf made of? How does a leaf grow? What purpose does a leaf serve?) First, however, Aristotle asks how *many* principles there are, and pauses briefly to refute the claim of Parmenides and his school, the Eleatics, that 'What is, is one and unchangeable.' Not that this monism is really the business of the student of nature, for whom it is an *assumption* that there are natural things and that they are subject to change. 'However, since these people, though they are not talking about nature, do raise difficulties that have to do with nature, it would perhaps be as well to say a little about them. The enquiry has some philosophical interest.'

Aristotle here grapples with an idea – that plurality and change are impossible and unreal – which has had a long and influential history, but which seemed to him (as to most of us) to be an absurdity based on deep misunderstandings. Some of these misunderstandings he will be dealing with in later books of the *Physics*. Here, in book I, he makes two simple but central points about the verb 'to be', in order to explode the thesis that what is is one. The first point is that 'things are said "*to be*" in many ways'. This simple assertion recurs at key points in Aristotle's metaphysics, and from it several of his most characteristic and fertile views develop. In our passage he uses it to introduce the point that things (i.e. substances, *ousiai*), qualities and quantities cannot all be said to be or to exist in the same sense. Qualities, for example, exist only as inhering in things, and to say that a quality exists is to say that a qualified thing exists. Dogs, colours, sizes, times and places do not belong in the same ontological drawer; and you will at once fall into absurdity if you speak about one of them in terms appropriate to another. (How heavy is yellow? Where is ten o'clock?) What, then, do the Eleatics really mean when they say that what is is one? Surely they cannot mean that there is nothing but substances – with no qualities or other characteristics? Or that there is nothing but qualities – floating around unowned by any substances? Or that there is just one single substance, without any qualities or other characteristics? Their thesis, when pressed, begins to seem quite unintelligible.

Besides being used against the monists, this idea that what there is divides into radically different types of item – the 'doctrine of the categories' – serves Aristotle well in a number of his own investigations. He is not dogmatic as to exactly how many categories should be distinguished; nor does he claim to give precise rules for settling borderline questions, for deciding cases where it is unclear into which of two categories some item belongs. What he does hold on to firmly is the broad division into substances, qualities, quantities and relations. He holds, no doubt rightly, that this division is fundamental to the world as we see and experience it, and that it is reflected in the ways in which we talk about the world.

A second and equally fundamental point about 'to be' is invoked by Aristotle against the monists. One of their key arguments depended on the supposition that if *x* and *y* are *two* items, *x* cannot *be y*. Relying on this they threw out all statements that ascribe characteristics to things or say that things change. For, they argue, any such statement as 'Tom is hot' must be false if 'Tom' and 'hot' name two different items – while if they name the same item the statement must be pointless (like 'Tom is Tom'). Moreover, if 'Tom is hot' were true, because 'Tom' and 'hot' named one and the same item, then it could not be true also to say 'Tom was not hot'; 'Tom was not hot but is hot' would be as absurd as 'Tom was not Tom but is Tom.' So all statements purporting to describe change go out of the window. Against all this Aristotle points out that 'is' does not always assert *identity*. It also, in fact usually, serves to ascribe a characteristic to something. Generosity and Tom are indeed *two* items (of different *types* or categories of course), but 'Tom is generous' does not say that these two different items are the same. It says that Tom *possesses*, not that he *is*, generosity. This is precisely the role in language of expressions like 'is generous' as opposed to 'is generosity'.

Thus Aristotle brings out, as is his wont, the implications of ordinary linguistic usage. He describes and distinguishes. He does not reform or strait-jacket, as some people at the time did, arguing that to use 'is' otherwise than for identity must be wrong and that the usage should be dropped. His remarks against the monists point forward to much sophisticated theorising (in Aristotle and still today) about kinds of predication, about identity, and about the forms of expression used to name or refer to or ascribe characteristics. What he does in the brief discussion of *Physics* I.2–3 is to put his finger on the most fundamental confusions in Eleatic philosophy – and to express the diagnosis with simple pungency.

Two other points, also pregnant with future applications, are touched on in these chapters of *Physics* I. First, within the class of identity-statements it is important to distinguish 'Tom is Tom' from 'Tom is the captain of the team.' Though 'the captain of the team' refers to Tom, it has a meaning of its own. To say that Tom and the captain of the cricket team are identical could easily lead to misunderstanding if it were overlooked that identity of reference and identity of meaning are different. (A further essential distinction is that between 'Tom is the captain of the team' and 'Tom is a man'; for it is clear that Tom might easily not have been the captain, but not at all clear that Tom might not have been a man. There is some sort of necessity about 'Tom is a man.') Secondly, there is the distinction between actuality and potentiality. A thing *can* after all be both one and many – and not only in the way in which Tom is one man but has many characteristics: it can be one *actually* and many *potentially* (e.g. an uncut cake), or one potentially and many actually (an un-made-up model-kit).

In Chapters 4–6 Aristotle draws upon the views and arguments of his predecessors to make plausible the view that change involves opposites and also something that underlies the opposites: the basic elements in change are three, the subject of change (what undergoes change), its character before the change, and its character after the change. Notice how different this account of basic 'elements' is from an account such as that given in the mid-fifth century BC by Empedocles, who said that the basic elements were four – earth, air, fire and water. *He* sought to identify the basic material stuffs; Aristotle here seeks the general structure of the very concept of change, he picks out the most elementary ideas involved in any talk of change.

In Chapter 7 Aristotle argues the matter out on his own behalf. The passage to be quoted is bound to read oddly in translation, because of certain features of the Greek language. In particular, the verb *gignesthai* can mean either 'come to be [such-and-such]' or 'come into being'; and the words translated 'the musical' could be used either for somebody who is musical or for the quality or state of being musical.

> When we say that one thing comes to be *from* another, or *from* something different, we may be talking either about what is simple or about what is compound. Let me explain. A man can come to be musical, but also the unmusical can come to be musical, or the unmusical man a musical man. I describe as *simple* the man and the unmusical (which comes to be) and the musical (which is what they come to be). When we say that the unmusical man comes to be a musical man, both the coming-to-be thing [the unmusical man] and that which it comes to be [the musical man] are *compound*.
>
> In some of these cases we say, not just that this comes to be, but that this comes to be from that – for example, a musical comes to be from an unmusical. But we do not speak in this way in all cases. We do not say that a musical comes to be from a man, but that the man comes to be musical.
>
> Of what we call the simple things which come to be, one remains when it comes to be, and the other does not. The man remains when he comes to be a musical man, but the unmusical does not remain, either by itself or as a component. (*Physics* I.7.189b32)

This passage is characteristic of Aristotle in two ways. First, it draws upon how we ordinarily speak. Aristotle assumes that how we speak will be a good guide to how things are, and he is extraordinarily acute in noting usages that have indeed proved of perennial philosophical interest. Secondly, the passage is a good example of the way in which Aristotle produces extremely general and abstract formulations backed up by just one or two standard examples. Here he is distinguishing two main forms of speech:

(i) x comes to be y
(ii) y comes to be from x.

And he also distinguishes different types of item that the x and the y may be:

(*a*) a simple item, e.g. a man, musical, unmusical
(*b*) a compound item, e.g. a musical man, an unmusical man.

He maintains that for some combinations of items form (ii) is not used. For example, a man becomes musical, but we do not say that musical comes to be from a man. More important, among simple items he contrasts those that remain when they become such-and-such, and those that do not remain – he contrasts the subject of change and the characteristic lost by that subject in the change. When the man becomes musical the man remains – it is the same man who before lacked and now has the knowledge of music; but the lack of knowledge no longer exists. So Aristotle goes on:

> It can be seen, then, in all cases of coming to be (if they are examined as we have suggested), that there must always be *something underlying* which is the coming-to-be thing; and this, even if it is one in number, is not one in form. (By 'in form' I mean the same as 'in account' or 'in definition'.) For being a man is not the same as being unmusical. And the one remains and the other does not. That which is not opposed remains – the man remains – but unmusical does not remain, and neither does the compound of the two, the unmusical man. (*Physics* I.7.190a13)

Aristotle now repeats a point already made, and also introduces an important type of case not yet mentioned.

> We say that something *comes to be from* something ... chiefly in connection with what does not remain. Thus we say that musical comes to be from unmusical [when the unmusical man becomes musical the unmusical 'does not remain', but is replaced by the musical], but we do not say that it comes to be from a man [the man remains]. However, we do sometimes speak in this way about things that remain: we say that a statue *comes to be from* bronze, not that bronze comes to be a statue. (*Physics* I.7.190a21)

The case Aristotle has in mind is where some material is made into a new thing, as a block of marble or a lump of bronze may be made into a statue. Consideration of such examples leads him to a new distinction, between one of the formulae already considered:

(i) *x* comes to be *y* [i.e. *x* becomes *y*]

and

(iii) *y* comes to be [i.e. *y* comes into being].

This last form of expression is appropriate where change brings into being a new *thing* (for example, a statue), not merely a new condition of the same pre-existing thing.

> Things are said to 'come to be' in many ways, and some things are said, not to come to be, but to come to be *something*, while only substances

are said simply to come to be [i.e. to come into being]. In other cases there must evidently be something underlying which is the coming-to-be thing – for when a quantity, quality, relation or place comes to be, it is *of* an underlying thing, since it is only substances that are not said of anything further, underlying them, whereas everything else is said of substances. (*Physics* I.7.190a31)

It is things – substances – that come into being, strictly speaking. They come into being *from* matter or material. When material is made into some sort of *thing*, that is a case of coming into being; but not when a thing merely undergoes a change of quality.

But that substances themselves, the things that simply *are*, come to be from something underlying, will become plain on consideration. For there is always something which underlies, from which the thing comes to be, as plants and animals come to be from seed. Some of the things which simply come to be, do so by change of shape (like a statue), some by addition (like things that grow), some by subtraction (as a figure of Hermes comes to be from the stone), some by composition (like a house), some by alteration (like things which change in respect of their matter). All things which come to be like this plainly come to be from underlying things. (*Physics* I.7.190b1)

Aristotle holds, then, that there are three principles involved in the analysis of *any* change – the underlying subject of change, its (pre-change) lack of a character, its (post-change) character. There are two main *types* of change: where the underlying subject is a definite thing, it first lacks and later acquires some characteristic – an unmusical man becomes a musical man; where what underlies the change is *material*, it is first unformed and later, from it, through the imposition of form, a thing of a definite kind comes into being – a chunk of marble is made into a statue.

Before commenting on the large questions that await Aristotle we may glance briefly at the next chapter, *Physics* I.8, in which he uses the conclusions just reached to resolve an old difficulty.

The first people to philosophise about the nature and truth of things got side-tracked and driven off course by inexperience. They said that nothing comes to be or passes away, because whatever comes to be must do so either from what is, or from what is not – and neither of these is possible. For what *is* cannot come to be, since it is already; and nothing can come to be from what is *not*, since there must [in all change and coming into being] be something underlying. (*Physics* I.8.191a24)

Aristotle's explanation of exactly how his analysis of change undermines this line of thought is not without difficulty, but it is clear that two main points are in play: (i) in the sense of 'from' in which a statue comes to be from stone, an object cannot come to be from what is not; the materials from which things are made, or which enable plants and animals to grow, must already be there. However, in the sense of 'from' in which knowledge comes from ignorance or shape from shapelessness, it is a *non*-existent, an absence, which change replaces by a positive characteristic. Only what is *not* such-and-such can *become* such-and-such. (ii) That which becomes a musical man is an unmusical man – and an unmusical man is something that *is* (a man), though *described* by reference to something that *is not* (musicality in him). So in a way the starting-point of change is what is, and in a way it is what is not.

Some problems

In *Physics* I, then, Aristotle has appealed to the various ways in which we ordinarily speak of change and of coming into being, in order to make clear the basic ideas involved and their interrelations, and to draw some distinctions that are necessary if puzzles about the possibility of change and generation are to be resolved. Before following him into his further study of the concepts and explanations used by students of nature, let us notice some of the problems thrown up by this discussion in Book I – problems to be handled more than once by Aristotle in the *Metaphysics* and elsewhere.

Things, materials and characteristics   Aristotle's analysis of change depends on two basic distinctions: the distinction between terms like 'man', which stand for persisting objects, and terms like 'musical', which ascribe characteristics to objects; and the distinction between terms like 'statue', which stand for objects, and terms like 'stone', which stand for materials. But how exactly, and with what justification, are these distinctions drawn? When a man becomes musical why *shouldn't* we say – not that one and the same thing, a man, first lacked and has now acquired a certain quality or characteristic, but – that a new thing, a musician, has come into being? Why should what I have done count as making a new thing [a table] if I have nailed some timber together, but not count as making a new thing if I have painted a table red? To put the question more generally, is our normal division of the world about us into things and characteristics purely arbitrary or conventional, or does it represent a real objective distinction? And since different languages classify things differently, and discriminate characteristics differently, can the particular way in which we in our language sort reality out into things (of various sorts) and characteristics (of various types) have any claim to objective validity? Aristotle certainly believes that the central features of ordinary language and thought are not just a matter of convention or convenience. In one area he relies upon a very important fact: 'A man begets a man, a musician does not beget a musician.' Plants and animals, living things, reproduce their kind, they are members of 'natural kinds'. Here, then, nature itself and not human convention shows that a line is to be drawn between man and musician. A musician is not a special kind of man, as a man is a special kind of animal; he is simply a man with a certain characteristic (knowledge of music). However, this biological point will not serve to justify all of the ways in which things are commonly contrasted with characteristics. In general Aristotle simply took for granted that Greek linguistic usage and habits of thought accurately and finally reflected objective reality. What he achieves, therefore, is a brilliant analysis of how the world looked to a Greek (and even looks perhaps to a Western European), but what he lacks is any recognition that to someone with quite another pair of spectacles the look might be utterly different. This is perhaps to say that he is Aristotle and not Kant.

I have raised a question about the distinction between things and characteristics. The same question can be raised about the distinction between materials and things. When gold is shaped, why *should* we say that a new thing, a ring, has been made, and not simply that one and the same thing, a piece of gold, first lacked and has now acquired a certain shape? Things are contrasted by Aristotle (and of course by us) both with what they are made of (their matter) and with the properties they have. But what, after all, *is* a 'thing' except matter with properties? Instead of treating things as the primary or basic entities, and matter and properties as somehow involved in them or belonging to them, we might do better to say that reality consists first and basically of matter and properties, and that talk of things (as opposed to matter and properties) comes later – that it is perhaps a great practical convenience but no more than that.

Essence and identity through time   Aristotle insists that in every change (whether movement in space or alteration in quality or size) *something remains the same*, the man, for example, or the gold. This is taken to be a necessary truth: it is part of the very concept of change that something or other undergoes it. (At one moment there is a Cheshire cat in the tree, a moment later there is a Cheshire cat on the ground. I shall not say that there has been a movement unless I suppose that it is the Cheshire cat which was in the tree that is now on the ground. If I entertain the idea – being in Wonderland – that the cat in the tree simply vanished out of existence and that soon after another cat simply came into existence, I shall be dropping the idea of 'something remaining the same' and hence dropping the idea that something has moved.) Two large questions now suggest themselves. Given that a man may change in all sorts of ways, is there some particular way in which he *cannot* change without ceasing to be a man? What exactly is involved in being a man, what is it to be a man, what is the *essence* of man? Secondly, if I met a man yesterday or last year and meet a man today, what am I claiming if I claim that it is the *same* man, and how can I hope to establish such a claim? Part of the claim presumably is that if I had accompanied yesterday's man or last year's man from then till now, following with him a continuous and uninterrupted path in space and time, I should now be standing beside *this* man. For we do not normally admit the idea that a man might disappear at one time and then reappear, the very same man, at a later time, or that he might disappear from one place and appear at the same time at another place. Another part of the claim must be that the man did not during the period in question undergo any such changes as would make him count as a different man. The problem here is often vividly expressed by reference to an artefact which undergoes patching and repair – like Sir John Cutler's famous silk stockings. 'These were darned with worsted until no particle of the silk was left in them, and no one could agree whether they were the same old stockings or were new ones.' At each stage they were a pair of stockings; there were no disappearances and reappearances. But can the pair he ended up with be properly called the same pair as he started with, given the complete change of material? In this case the question may seem trivial and silly. But where the identity of a *man* is concerned serious consequences may follow from one decision or the other. If Dr Jekyll could persuade us that he was not the same man as Mr Hyde, he would escape punishment for the crimes of his *alter ego*.

Matter and form   According to Aristotle a generated thing – natural or artificial – is material on which form has been imposed. In a simple example the idea seems clear enough, but difficulties arise when it is pushed further and applied more widely. Thus, the golden ring is some gold shaped in a certain way. But that gold was itself a generated *compound*: gold is such and such elements [matter] combined in a certain way [form]. What about the elements themselves? Aristotle thought that there were just four basic elements (earth, water, air and fire), and that each was characterised by a pair of properties (each being either hot or cold and either wet or dry). He thought that one element could change into another, by a change in one of the characteristics; the hot–dry element, for example, would change into the cold–dry element if it lost heat and became cold. But now, if these changes are to be possible, each *element* must itself be a compound of 'prime matter', matter with no characteristics, and two of the basic characteristics. Is such a notion of 'prime matter' intelligible? (Berkeley was to mock Locke in the eighteenth century on the grounds that he was committed to just such an 'unknowable substrate'.) It is a matter of dispute whether Aristotle's use of the form–matter distinction does in fact commit him to the actual existence of prime matter, or whether in his hands it is only an analytical device leading to no such metaphysical puzzles.

A corresponding difficulty arises at the top end of the scale. A given material can be formed into something of a higher level, and that again can be further organised or formed. Stone is shaped into blocks, with blocks walls are built, walls and roofs make houses; at each stage a higher degree of form or organisation is imposed. Can there be such a thing as pure form without matter – or would this be a quite unintelligible suggestion? Can Aristotle say that matter and form can be distinguished in everything, as aspects of everything, without having to claim that there could be matter without form and form without matter?

A final illustration of the perplexities into which the matter–form contrast leads may be found in its application to the mind–body problem, or the soul–body problem. When Aristotle tells us that the soul is the form of the body we are very far from the easy case of the carpenter making a table, and we are not sure how to understand him. (See pages 68–78.)

We have seen that our ordinary ways of speaking and thinking about things and changes raise many difficult questions, and that there are many problems in understanding Aristotle's analysis. Some of these will be discussed further in later chapters (especially Chapters 5 and 9). But it will be useful next to outline the second book of the *Physics*, in which Aristotle tries to explain more clearly what things natural philosophy is about, and what kinds of question about them it seeks to answer.

4 Explanation in natural science

Nature, matter and form

Most of what Aristotle has said in *Physics* I about things and changes applies to all changeable things, including man-made artefacts. The student of nature, however, is not concerned with all changeable things, but only with natural ones. So in *Physics* II.2 Aristotle proceeds to offer an account of *nature*: 'nature is a sort of source and cause of changing (and of remaining unchanged) in that to which it belongs primarily and of itself – that is, not incidentally'. Thus any natural object – a lump of iron, for example, or a plant or an animal – has its own characteristic way of acting and reacting. How an artefact behaves, on the other hand, depends entirely on the characteristics of its *natural* constituents. The natural powers an axe has belong to it not 'of itself' – because it is an axe – but only 'incidentally', i.e. because it is made of wood and iron; wood, however, and iron do have natural powers of their own, 'of themselves'.

This way of drawing the distinction between natural objects and artefacts leaves something to be desired. How an axe behaves does not depend only on its material constituents and their powers, but also on its structure, how the constituents are put together, the *form* that makes them into an axe. In the same way, the natural behaviour of (say) a plant, its characteristic way of acting and reacting, presumably depends on the powers of its material constituents, as well as on the way in which they are compounded or formed. If so, then whether a thing is natural or an artefact it will in either case behave as it does because of (i) what it is made of, and (ii) how it is put together; and Aristotle's way of distinguishing them seems to break down. He may of course think that *natural* objects have certain characteristics which are not deducible from their ingredients and structure – 'emergent' characteristics – whereas artificial objects have none. He may think, in other words, that all the properties and powers of an axe could be calculated in advance by anyone who knew what materials it was to be made of and how they were to be put together, but that nobody could deduce all of an animal's living powers simply from knowledge of its physical and chemical structure. It is tempting to suppose that there is indeed a sharp distinction of this kind between the animate and the inanimate, and that life and mind are in this sense 'emergent' powers. But whether this is true or not, it is not clear that the distinction will serve to explain the ordinary contrast we draw between natural things and artefacts.

The analysis of change showed that in any changeable object matter and form can be distinguished. Aristotle now asks whether the nature of a natural object – its inner 'source of change' – resides in its matter or in its form. Is it its form or its matter that explains its characteristic way of acting and reacting? Let us see how Aristotle argues the case, first on behalf of matter.

Some people think that the nature and real being [*ousia*] of a natural object is the primary material in it (material in itself unformed) – in a bed it would be the wood, in a statue the bronze. It is an indication of this, according to Antiphon, that if you bury a bed, and the rotting wood becomes able to send up a shoot, what comes up will not be a bed, but wood – suggesting that the arrangement in accordance with the rules of the art belongs only incidentally, and that the reality – what the thing really is – is what actually persists through all those changes.

If the various materials are themselves similarly related to something else – if, for example, bronze and gold are so related to water, and bone and wood to earth, and so on – the thing to which they are so related is *their* nature and real being. That is why fire, earth, air and water (one, some or all of them) have been held to be the real nature of all the things there are, and everything else to be affections or states or dispositions of them . . .

This then is one way in which we may speak of *nature* – as the primary underlying matter, in each case, of things which have in themselves a source of movement and change. (*Physics* II.1.193a9)

Next, Aristotle offers some arguments in favour of regarding its form as a thing's nature.

But there is another way of speaking, according to which the nature of a thing is its shape or form as given in its definition . . . and this rather than its matter is a thing's nature. For (i) each thing is called whatever it is, when it is that thing actually rather than just potentially [the wood or the seed, the matter, *is* not a table or a lettuce – though it may have the potentiality of being one – until it has actually been put together or has actually germinated and grown]. Further, (ii) men come to be from men, but not beds from beds. That is precisely why people say that the nature of a bed is not the shape but the wood; if it sprouts it is not a bed but wood that comes up. But if this shows that the wood is nature,

form too is nature; for men come to be from men. [Finally, Aristotle
has an etymological argument.] (iii) The word for 'nature' is connected
with the word for 'growth', and in growth things acquire their nature;
but what they acquire in growth – like the wood being made into a
table – is *form*. (*Physics* II.1.193a30)

Many difficult questions about matter and form remain to be discussed.
For the present Aristotle insists only that the natural scientist must study
both. 'If art imitates nature, and the same branch of knowledge has to
know both the form and the matter (up to a point) – as for example the
doctor has knowledge of health, but also of bile and phlegm (materials in
which health resides), and the builder knows the form of a house and also
the matter (that it is bricks and timbers) – it follows that the student of
nature has to know both sorts of nature.' It is typical of Aristotle that he
does not accept the crude dichotomy expressed in the question 'Is a
thing's nature its matter *or* its form?' The word 'nature' can be used in
both ways, there is something to be said on both sides; to gain a full
understanding the scientist will have to deal with both form and matter.

Types of explanation

But there are other questions for the scientist, besides 'What is it made
of?' and 'What is its shape, structure, form?' A natural object, like an
artefact, is brought into being by certain processes. So he must ask 'What
brought it about?' (just as we ask 'Who made the table?'). Moreover, if
the analogy with artefacts holds, there will be a question about the
purpose or function of the natural object (parallel to the question 'What
is a table *for*?'). In the third chapter of *Physics* II Aristotle tries to
enumerate and to classify all the kinds of question that may be raised, all
the types of explanation that may be sought. This is his celebrated (or
notorious) 'doctrine of the four causes'. It might better be called a
doctrine of the four 'becauses': Aristotle is distinguishing different sorts
of answer that can be given to the question 'Why?' or 'Because of what?'
Only one of them, the one he calls 'the source of the change' –
traditionally called the 'efficient cause' – comes at all close to our
common use of the term 'cause'. Much unjustified criticism of Aristotle's
doctrine would have been avoided if the word 'cause' had not been used
in translations, but it has become traditional and no other single word
does better. In reading what follows, therefore, remember that the four
so-called 'causes' are *types of explanatory factor*. Aristotle's suggestion is
that a full knowledge and understanding of anything requires a grasp of
all four.

These distinctions having been drawn, we must ask how many sorts of cause there are, and what they are like. For since the aim of our investigation is knowledge, and we do not think we have knowledge of a thing until we have grasped *why* it is (*because of* what), we must clearly do this about coming to be and passing away and all natural change; so that, knowing their principles, we may try to bring each object of enquiry back to them.

[(i) 'Material cause':] According to one way of speaking, that from which as a constituent a thing comes to be is called a cause; for example, the bronze and the silver (and their genera) would be the causes respectively of a statue and a loving-cup. [(ii) 'Formal cause':] According to another, the *form* or model is a cause; this is the account of what it is to be a so-and-so (and its genera), e.g. the cause of an octave is the ratio of two to one (and more generally number). [(iii) 'Efficient cause':] Again, there is the primary *source of the change* (or of the staying unchanged). For example, the man who has deliberated is a cause [of his actions], the father is a cause of the child, and in general what makes something is a cause of what is made, and what changes something of what is changed. [(iv) 'Final cause':] And again, there is the end, what something is for, as health might be what a walk is for. 'Why does he walk?' We answer 'To keep fit'; and we think that we have given the cause. The same is true of everything which, once the change has been started, comes about on the way to the end, as slimming, purging, drugs and surgical instruments come about as means to health: all of these are for the end, though they differ in that some are things done and others are things used.

Causes then are spoken of in these various ways. This being so, it follows that several different things can all be causes of the same thing (and not just incidentally). For instance, both the art of statue-making and the bronze are causes of a statue (and causes of it, not in so far as it is anything else, but *as* a statue); they are not, however, causes in the same *way*, but the latter is a cause as matter, and the former as that from which the change proceeds. Some things are even causes of each other; for example, exercise is the cause of good condition, and good condition of exercise – not, however, in the same way, but the one is a cause as end, and the other as source of change. (*Physics* II.3.194b16)

Having distinguished these four sorts of fact or explanation, and having claimed that all four are needed for a complete understanding of anything, Aristotle makes some remarks about the correct formulation of explanations. First, one must not give as an explanation what is a cause only 'incidentally': if Callias the cook has baked a pastry and Callias is an uncle, it is *not* appropriate to say (when giving the 'source of the change') that an *uncle* has baked the pastry. Secondly, even to say 'Callias baked the pastry' is not to give the primary cause – for it was not qua Callias but qua cook that he did it; nothing peculiar to him as Callias was involved. His being Callias does not help to explain anything. So we ought rather to say that it was a *cook* who baked the pastry. Finally, it was strictly not as a cook simply, but as a *pastry*-cook that he baked the pastry. It is his being a pastry-cook that explains his being able to plan and carry out the making of the pastry. Thus though there are numerous true statements which can be made about the episode in question, the strictly formulated account of the 'efficient cause' of the pastry is one that refers to a *pastry-cook*.

This may all seem rather absurd, and the example I have used may seem suitable for *Alice in Wonderland* rather than for a serious philosophical treatise. However there are important points being made, as indeed there often are in *Alice in Wonderland*. First, there is a general logical point that Aristotle was the first to recognise clearly and to exploit: in some sorts of statement, though not in all, exactly *how* somebody or something is described or referred to makes a crucial difference to the truth or falsity of what is said. (This is a point now recognised to be of the greatest importance for many questions in philosophical logic and the philosophy of language.) Suppose that the cook is the chairman of the local Liberal party. If it is true to say 'The cook has a cold', it is true to say 'The chairman has a cold.' It does not matter which you say, since you are referring to one and the same person in both cases, though referring to him in different ways. Suppose, however, that the cook has been dismissed; it by no means follows that you can truly say 'The chairman has been dismissed.' The chairman may well have been receiving a vote of confidence at the very moment when the cook was being given the sack. Again, the road from Reading to Caversham *is* the road from Caversham to Reading. Yet the road from Reading to Caversham is uphill, while the road from Caversham to Reading is downhill. Aristotle has two main ways to mark this sort of distinction. He sometimes says that *a* and *b* are 'the same, but different in *logos* [description or definition]': the cook and the chairman are one and the same person, but referred to under two different descriptions. He sometimes uses the phrase we translate by the Latin 'qua': qua cook the man has been dismissed, qua chairman he has been re-elected.

Secondly, in explanations – including what we ourselves should call causal explanations – it really is desirable to give the explanation that fully and precisely accounts for the thing or phenomenon in question. If my roses suffer from wilt I do not want to be told that the wilt is due to a pest; I want to know exactly what pest causes this particular condition. A scientist wishes to be able to say with respect to an event or phenomenon *x* that it was due to certain preceding and concomitant events or conditions *a*, *b*, *c*, *d*, a claim that carries the implication that precisely such events or conditions always produce precisely an *x*-phenomenon. After all, he has not explained the measles if the events or conditions he mentions always produce a *disease* but not always measles; nor is it the correct explanation if, although the factors he mentions do always produce measles, they are not the only factors that do so. The proper, adequate explanation of measles must be 'commensurate': whenever the explanation holds, there is measles, *and* whenever there is measles, the explanation holds.

While this demand for a 'commensurate' explanation is justified and important, it must be allowed that Aristotle's way of responding to it smacks of triviality. To insist that it is a pastry-maker who made the pastry meets the demand rather too easily. By the same token the efficient cause of any item *x* will have to be an *x*-maker. But to say this is no more illuminating than it would be to tell me that my roses' wilt is due to a wilt-producer and my child's measles to a measles-producer. It is not that we expect the scientist to be able to identify and point out to us the *individual* agents, the individual insect responsible for our roses' wilt, the individual germ responsible for our child's measles; for the scientist is concerned with *general* truths. But he should surely be able to identify and characterise what produces wilt or measles in such a way as to make it possible for us to go out and identify individual agents in particular cases; and this requires more of him than that he should say 'wilt-producer', 'measles-producer'.

In the next chapters (II.4–6) Aristotle works out an acute analysis of luck and chance. Many things are certainly thought to come about because of them, and if asked why something happened we can reply 'By luck' or 'By chance.' We must therefore ask whether they really *are* causes, and, if so, how they are related to the four mentioned above. The two main elements Aristotle finds in the idea of luck are absence of regularity and absence of deliberate intention. He relies on this sort of example: if you go to the market to buy food and happen to meet a man who owes you money – when to collect the debt was not your motive for going, and when the man is not a regular market-goer – that is your good luck. Luck, then, is 'an incidental cause of what is for something [i.e. serves a purpose], in the area of choice'. Chance is a wider idea, applying where there could not possibly have been any question of deliberate choice. It was by luck that you recovered the money from your debtor – you might well have set out deliberately to find him, though in fact you went to the market to do your shopping. It was by chance that the boulder fell in such a way as to form a convenient seat – this outcome almost looks as though it had been intended, but there is not really any suggestion that the boulder might well have planned this though in fact it didn't. Nor, of course, do boulders regularly fall like that; it is no part of a boulder's nature to fall into a seat-like position.

Aristotle concludes from his analysis that 'chance and luck are posterior to both mind and nature; so however much chance may be the cause of the heavens, mind and nature are necessarily prior causes both of many other things and of this universe'. Luck and chance, he is claiming, *presuppose* patterns of normal, regular, goal-directed action ('mind and nature'); and so it would be absurd to suggest that *everything* happens by luck and chance. We can have reason to say that some things happen as if they had been planned only because we take for granted that some things happen because they have really been planned; and we can pick out certain sequences as irregular and exceptional only against the background of sequences that are regular and to be expected.

Aristotle is here trying to draw important conclusions about how things are from points about how we speak and think. How much such considerations can actually prove is not always easy to decide. With Aristotle's claims about luck, chance and regularity one may compare the following modern arguments. (i) It is absurd to suggest that one is the only person there is ('solipsism'). For the idea of oneself as a person can have been developed only along with the idea of other persons. So the very statement of the suggestion implies its own falsity. (ii) It is absurd to suggest that no actions are ever really free. For we could not have learnt to apply the word 'free' to actions at all if there were never any examples of free action. Only in contrast to some actions that are free can we pick out others that are not.

In the next chapter (II.7) Aristotle moves from the doctrine of four causes towards the idea of just two radically different types of explanation, one appealing to necessity and one to teleology or 'what a thing is for'. He says that the efficient, formal and final causes often coincide, so that an enquiry into what a thing is for will reveal all of them; while the study of the material cause is the study of the necessary conditions for the coming into being of a natural object.

That the efficient and formal causes are in a way the same is an idea foreshadowed in the previous discussion. It is a pastry-cook that makes pastry; or, to go even further, the 'source of the change' is the thought of pastry in the pastry-cook's mind. Thus in the case of artefacts it is (the thought of) a so-and-so that produces a so-and-so. In the case of living things it is an actual so-and-so that produces a so-and-so. The other idea, that formal and final cause coincide – that what a thing *is* is what it is for –

will call for further discussion later. Now only two preliminary remarks: (i) it is clearer that a carving-knife is defined by its work or purpose than that a tree is. (What *is* the work or purpose of a tree?) (ii) What is the relation or connection between what something is for, or what it does, and its structure – its shape, organisation of parts, etc.? If the latter is its form as opposed to its matter (as we have often said), how can it be identified with what it is for? How can a structure be identical with a function?

Teleology

In the next chapter (II.8) Aristotle begins by stating a non-teleological view of natural history, a view according to which nothing is directed to an end or happens because it is best that it should, but everything is a matter of chance and necessity. He then develops a series of arguments against that view.

> Why should we suppose that nature does act 'for' something and because it is better? Why should not everything be like the rain? Zeus does not send the rain in order to make the corn grow; it comes of necessity. The vapour that has been drawn up is bound to cool, and, having cooled, to turn into water and come down. That the corn grows when this has happened is merely incidental. Similarly, if someone's corn rots on the threshing-floor, it is not *for* this that it rained – in order that the corn should rot; that just comes about incidentally. So why should it not be the same with parts in nature also – the front teeth *of necessity* growing sharp and suitable for biting, and the back teeth broad and useful for chewing food, not coming to be *for* this, but this was just incidental? And similarly with the other parts in which purpose seems to be present. So where all the parts turned out just as if they had come to be something, these things survived, suitably put together by chance; otherwise they died, and do die (as Empedocles says the man-headed calves did).
>
> Such a line of thought may well give us pause. Yet it is not possible that this should really be how things are.

The first main argument goes: nature exhibits great regularity, whereas chance by definition involves an absence of regularity, as we saw above. So what happens naturally cannot be a matter of chance, and must therefore be purposive – 'for something'.

> For the things mentioned, and all things that are by nature, either always come to be in the same way or usually, whereas nothing that happens by luck or chance does so. We do not think that it is by luck

or coincidence that there is a lot of rain in winter, but only if there is a lot of rain in midsummer; nor that there are heat waves in midsummer, but only if there is a heat wave in winter. So if, as it seems, things are either a coincidental result or for something, and the things we are discussing cannot be coincidental or a result of chance, they must be for something. But they are certainly natural – as our opponents themselves admit. The 'for something', then, is present in things that are, and come to be, by nature.

The second main argument – or group of arguments – appeals to the analogy between nature and human arts and crafts.

Again, wherever there is an end, it is for this that the previous things are done, one after the other. Now as things are done, so they occur by nature, and as they occur by nature, so they are done, if there is no impediment. But things are done *for* something. Therefore by nature also they occur *for* something. Thus if a house were one of the things that come to be by nature, it would come to be just as it now does by the agency of art; and if natural things came to be not only by nature but also by art, they would come to be just as they do by nature. What comes first is for the sake of what comes later. In general, art either perfects what nature cannot bring to completion or imitates nature. Clearly, therefore, if what is in accordance with art is for something, what is in accordance with nature is also for something, since the relation of what comes after to what goes before is the same in both.

The point is most obvious if you consider animals other than men, which make things not by art, and without enquiries or deliberation – so that people ask whether it is by intelligence or by something else that spiders, ants and the like accomplish what they do. Going a little further, in plants too you see things coming to be which serve an end, for instance leaves for the protection of fruit. So if it is both by nature and for something that the swallow makes its nest and the spider its web, and plants have leaves for the sake of the fruit, and send roots not up but down for nourishment, this sort of cause is evidently present in things that are and come to be by nature. And since nature is twofold – nature as matter and nature as form – and the latter is an end, and everything else is for the end, the cause as that *for* which must be the latter, the form.

Of course, nature does not always get it right and achieve its goal, but nor does a craftsman. And nature does not, of course, deliberate, but nor does the thoroughly skilled craftsman.

Mistakes occur even in the arts. Men who can write may write incorrectly, a doctor may give the wrong medicine. So clearly the same is possible too in natural things. If it sometimes happens in the arts, that what goes right is for something, while what goes wrong is aiming at something but miscarries, it may be the same with things in nature, monsters being unsuccessful attempts at what is for something. When things were originally being put together, man-headed calves, if they were unable to reach a certain limit and end, came into being because some principle was defective, as such things do now because of defective seed . . .

It is absurd to think that things come to be *for* something only if what brings about the change is seen to have deliberated. After all, art itself does not deliberate. If the art of shipbuilding were present in wood, it would act in the same way as nature; so if the 'for something' is present in art, it is present in nature too. The point is clearest when someone doctors himself; nature is like that.

That nature is a cause, then, and a cause as being *for* something, is plain.

What are we to think of these arguments for teleology in nature? We do often take regularity to be a sign of purpose and to exclude the merely random: if we notice that our neighbour always wears a suit and takes the car to work on Mondays and Wednesdays, but wears a sports jacket and cycles on every other day, we suppose there to be some reason for this. But on other occasions we may speak of 'mechanical' necessity, implying that what always happens in the same way – in accordance with 'natural laws' – is precisely *not* designed or intended for a purpose. The obvious distinction is between the case where a conscious, rational agent is in question – someone who can deliberate and have reasons and act to achieve his aims – and cases where there is no such agent. Against this Aristotle argues that the absence of deliberation in nature does not prove an absence of purposiveness, because after all a skilled craftsman need not deliberate about how to proceed. (Indeed, the more skilled he is, the less he has to think out what to do.) To this we may reply that the skilled craftsman *could* always explain to us why he is doing what he does, even if he had no need to work it out; and that *that* is why we regard him as a rational agent capable of purposive action, but do not regard nature or spiders in the same way.

But suppose we encounter somebody unable or unwilling to explain to us? We shall still ascribe purposes to him, provided that we can understand what he is up to, provided that we can interpret what he does in terms of beliefs and desires that we share or at least comprehend. But once we have got to this point, why should we *not* ascribe purposes to animals and plants, and to their parts, if, as is often the case, we can see how certain activities or performances serve their needs and preserve their life? In biology and medicine scientists study how an animal's organs work to maintain the life of the animal – as well as how they grow and develop from birth; they investigate the point and purpose of activities (such as the bees' dance) – as well as how they are performed. Discovering what the organ or the activity is *for* is more than discovering what regularly happens; it involves discovering the connection between this organ or activity and what other parts do, and how they all contribute to the whole life of the animal. So the general idea of certain things in nature being *for* something is clear enough, and acceptable.

However, serious objections and difficulties remain: (i) we surely cannot accept Aristotle's contention that *everything* that happens regularly is *for* something, that regularity proves purposiveness. In an animal we select from all the regularities those that contribute to the preservation of the animal, and say that *they* are *for* something, serve a purpose. Many other regularities seem to be simply law-governed chemical or physical processes that may serve no purpose. This is a distinction which Aristotle himself elsewhere allows and makes, and he deals with these *non*-purposive regularities in one of two ways. Some of them may be seen as necessities which underly and are presupposed by the purposive performances. A craftsman could not carry out his skilful plans if there were not various materials behaving in certain definite ways – reliable regularities capable of being exploited and being turned to good (or bad) use. So the notion of purpose and purposive regularities positively requires there to be some non-purposive or pre-purposive regularities. Alternatively, some non-purposive regularities may be seen as accidental concomitants or results of purposive performances. When my cat drinks milk he gets his whiskers wet. He drinks milk twice a day and (consequently) gets his whiskers wet twice a day. His regular milk-drinking serves an obvious purpose, but his regular whisker-wetting serves none; it is a non-purposive concomitant of a purposive regularity.

(ii) Granted that we can explain the function of some part or activity by reference to the preservation of the whole animal, does it make sense to speak of the function of the animal as a whole? Does it and its life serve a purpose? 'What is a sheep-dog for?' can be answered – by reference to the shepherd's needs and desires. But 'What is dog for?' sounds odd, as odd as 'What is a star for?' Aristotle has two moves at his disposal. First, by insisting that the individual dog is a member of the species dog he provides something beyond the individual that the individual life does help to preserve. The point of a dog's life is to maintain the species, by living a canine life and bringing on a new generation. (But now: What is the species itself for?) Secondly, Aristotle sees every kind of thing in the universe as imitating in its own way the changeless activity of god: the stars do so by constant circular motion, animals by maintaining themselves and their species, elements (like earth and air) by constantly displaying their basic properties. So everything is 'for' god – not in the sense that he benefits, but in the sense that everything that happens in the universe can be understood only as strivings towards something unchanging and eternal. We shall return to this idea in Chapter 9.

Necessity

In the last chapter of *Physics* II Aristotle explains the sort of *necessity* to be found in nature and likens it to that in arts and crafts. He admits that certain conditions are necessary *if* some desirable result is to be produced ('hypothetical necessity'), but denies that from such conditions such results necessarily follow ('absolute necessity'). Thus the characteristics and behaviour of materials do not themselves bring about the artefact; rather, the artist uses and exploits them to serve his purpose. A builder cannot make a wall *without* bricks and mortar and their characteristics, but bricks and mortar do not by themselves build a wall. To understand walls and wall-building one must know all about bricks and mortar, how they can be made and put together. But, more important still, one must know what walls are for, and the ways in which various types of structure can serve various purposes. Similarly the student of nature must certainly understand the underlying necessities (the characteristics and behaviour of materials, and how the relevant physical processes take place), but he must not suppose that they give a full explanation of natural objects, or even explain what is most important about them

Is what is necessary, necessary on some hypothesis, or can it also be unconditionally necessary? People suppose that there is necessity in what comes to be, as a man might think that a city wall had come to be necessarily, because heavy things are by nature such as to sink down, and light things such as to rise to the surface – which is why the stones and foundations go down, the earth goes above them because it is lighter, and the posts go on top because they are lightest of all. In fact, however, though the wall has not come to be *without* these materials, it was not because of them, except as its matter, that it has come to be, but for protecting and preserving certain things. Similarly with anything else in which a purpose is present: without the things which have a necessary nature it could not be, but it is not because of them, except as being its matter, but for something. For example, why is a saw like this [i.e. of such a shape, size and material]? So that it may be a saw, a thing for sawing. It is impossible, however, for this, which it is for, to come to be, unless it is made of iron. It is necessary, then, for it to be made of iron, *if* it is to be a saw, and do its work. So it is on some hypothesis ['*if* it is to be a saw'] that the necessary is necessary, and not as an end. For the necessity is in the matter [i.e. it is the matter that *must* be of a certain sort], while that for the sake of which [the matter has to be of a certain sort] is in the definition [i.e. the form to be realised]. (*Physics* II.9.199b34)

Aristotle has identified a thing with its form, i.e. its function; and he has claimed that its material composition is explained by that. However, full understanding does call for knowledge of matter as well as form, and a complete definition or account of anything will therefore have to refer to both – as he goes on to say.

Perhaps however the necessary does enter the definition too. If we define the work of a saw as a certain kind of dividing, that will not be possible unless the saw has teeth of a certain sort, and it will not have these teeth unless it is made of iron. Thus certain parts of the definition or account of the thing are as it were the *material* side of the definition. (*Physics* II.9.200b4)

Illustrations from the biological works

It is in the biological works in particular that we find Aristotle actually giving explanations of the types indicated in the above passages; and it is to them that we must look if we want to get a fuller idea of his teleology and to see how his theory of scientific explanation works out in practice. So before making some further remarks about teleology and necessity I should like to give a few illustrative passages from Aristotle's treatise *On the Parts of Animals*.

In the first passage Aristotle argues that since the bodily organs serve certain purposes, the body as a whole must do so. Eyes are for seeing, the body as a whole is 'for' the animal's life as a whole.

Now, as each of the parts of the body, like every tool or instrument, is for the sake of some thing, namely some action, it is evident that the body as a whole also exists for the sake of some action, a complex one. The saw is there for the sake of sawing and not sawing for the sake of the saw, because sawing is the using of the instrument. So too the body exists for the sake of the soul, and the parts of the body for the sake of the various functions it is their nature to perform. (*Parts of Animals* I.5.645b15)

In the next passage Aristotle claims that natural processes, like those in arts and skills, are explained by the goals which they reach rather than by their early stages. Indeed in a way the goals are *before* the processes, in that what sets off the process leading to a new house is a house (the house in the thoughts of the architect), and what sets off the process leading to a new man is himself a man (the father). So to explain the process of coming into being of an *x* it is necessary to refer to an *x* existing (in thought or in fact) before the process in question. To put the point in another way: to define the process of house-building you have to take for granted knowledge of what a house is, while you can define what a house is without assuming any knowledge of house-building.

Now the order of development is the reverse of the real order. What is later in the formative process is earlier by its nature, and what comes at the end of the process is first by its nature. Thus a house, though it comes after the bricks and stone, is not there for the sake of them, they are there for the sake of the house [so the house is 'first by its nature']. And the same applies to materials of every kind.

That this is how things are is clear if one considers examples; but it can also be shown by a general argument. Everything that comes into being is coming out of something [material] to something [the final product or grown animal], and from one principle towards another, from the primary moving cause which already has a certain nature, towards a certain form or other such end. For example, a man begets a man and a plant begets a plant, out of the underlying material in each case. Thus, matter and the process of formation come first in time, but in *logos* [account or definition] the essence [*ousia*] and form of the thing must be first. This is clear if we state the *logos* of the process. For example, the *logos* of the process of house-building includes the *logos* of a house, whereas that of a house does not include that of the process of house-building. And this holds good in all such cases. (*Parts of Animals* II.1.646a25)

Aristotle goes on to apply this idea to the development of the whole animal. In its growth simpler parts were first, structures of greater complexity come later – but they and the final developed body are what the earlier processes are for. It is the eventual rich variety of the animal's life – his soul – that explains his complex body, and it is the final complex body that explains the earlier gradual processes of growth and development (and the particular materials involved). Now for some particular examples. Notice the two types of explanation, that in terms of function or the good and that in terms of material process or the necessary.

Human hair   Man has the hairiest head of all the animals. First, this is *necessarily* so because of the fluidity of his brain and the sutures in his skull. For there must necessarily be the largest outgrowth where there is most fluid and heat. Secondly, it is for giving protection, so that the hair may give shelter and protection from excesses of cold and heat. The human brain, being the biggest and the most fluid of all, needs the greatest amount of protection, since the more fluid a thing is the more liable is it to excessive heating or chilling. (*Parts of Animals* II.14.658b2)

Eyebrows and eyelashes   Both eyebrows and eyelashes exist for the protection of the eyes. The eyebrows, like the eaves of a house, give protection from the fluids running down from the head; the eyelashes, like the palisades sometimes put up in front of an enclosure, are there to keep out things that might get in. The eyebrows are at the junction of two bones – which is why they often get so thick in old age that they have to be cut. The eyelashes are at the ends of small blood-vessels. For these vessels come to an end where the skin itself terminates. At these places the moisture that comes off, being corporeal, must necessarily cause the formation of hairs, unless it is diverted by nature to some other use. (*Parts of Animals* II.15.658b14)

Here are other examples of the same kind. That serpents can roll up and turn their heads backwards is a *necessary* consequence of their structure (their vertebrae are cartilaginous and flexible), but it serves a *good* purpose too, enabling them to guard against attacks from the rear. Web-feet in water-birds are a *necessary* consequence of the processes of growth, but it is also *better* that they should have such feet, which are useful in enabling them to swim.

In the following discussion of the elephant's trunk notice the reference to the animal's environment: since he lives in swamps he has to have such-and-such if he is to be able to breath and feed. This is very close to the evolutionist's way of speaking: unless he had means of breathing and feeding in swamps he would not have survived in swamps. Notice also in this example the idea that a part essential for one purpose may also serve a second purpose.

The elephant's trunk   The elephant's nose [his trunk] is unique owing to its extraordinary size and strength. It is by means of his trunk, as if by a hand, that the elephant conveys his food, both solid and fluid, to his mouth. It is with it that he tears up trees, by coiling it round them. He uses it, in fact, just as if it were a hand. For the elephant is by his nature both a land-animal and a swamp-dweller. So he had to get his food from the water; yet he had to breathe (since he is a land-animal and has blood); but owing to his enormous size could not transfer himself quickly from the water on to the land (as do quite a number of blooded viviparous animals that breathe). It was therefore necessary for him to be equally at home on land and in the water. Now sea-divers are sometimes provided with breathing-apparatus, through which they can inhale air from above the surface and so remain for a long time in the water. Nature has provided the elephant with such an apparatus – his long trunk. Whenever he makes his way through deep water, he lifts his trunk up to the surface and breathes through it. For, as we have said, the elephant's trunk is a nose.

Now it would have been impossible for the trunk to be like this if it had not been soft and able to bend; otherwise its very length would have prevented the animal from getting its food (just as they say the horns of the 'backward-grazing' oxen do, forcing them to walk backwards as they feed). So the trunk is soft and flexible. And nature, as is its wont, finds an extra job for it to do, the job – in other animals – of the forefeet. For in other quadrupeds the forefeet serve as hands as well as supports, but the elephant is so large and heavy that his forefeet can serve only as supports; they are no good for anything else because they move so slowly and cannot easily bend.

So the elephant's trunk is there, in the first place, to enable him to breathe (as in all animals that have a lung); and also it is lengthened and able to coil itself round things because the elephant spends much of his time in the water and cannot quickly get out on to land. And as he is limited in the use of his feet, nature makes further use of the trunk to provide the help that should have been given by them. (*Parts of Animals* II.16.658b33)

Here is another case of one organ with two jobs, but here one job is of a higher order than the other: one helps the animal to survive, the other promotes his well-being.

The lips In all animals except man the lips are simply to preserve and to protect the teeth. Man's lips are soft and fleshy and can be separated, and they are there not only to protect his teeth, but – still more important – to promote his well-being, since they help to make possible his use of speech. Compare the way in which the human tongue, which is unlike that of any other animal, is used by nature for two jobs (a device of hers which we have often noted), for tasting and for speech. Now speech consists of combinations of various sounds, some of which are produced by an impact of the tongue, some by closing the lips; and if the lips were not supple, or if the tongue were other than it is, most of these sounds could not possibly be made. (*Parts of Animals* II.16.659b27)

Sometimes, Aristotle admits, natural processes have results that serve no purpose. Here is one example.

The bile The bile around the liver, as well as elsewhere in the body, seems to be a mere residue or waste product, and not to be *for* anything. Sometimes, it is true, nature turns even residues to use; but that does not mean that one should look for a purpose in all cases. Because there are certain constituents of a certain character, many others are necessary in consequence. (*Parts of Animals* IV.11.677a13)

Here is another slightly different example. That animals should have eyes is of course necessary if they are to see and to survive – eyes are obviously 'for' the good. But what colour the eyes are makes no difference; the particular colour is a side-consequence of the physical processes of growth. The colour, like a useless waste product, is a necessary consequence without any usefulness of its own.

As a last example I mention Aristotle's treatment of two questions about the growth of teeth. Why are the front teeth formed first and the molars afterwards? And why are the molars not shed, whereas the front teeth are, and new ones grow? He explains these facts by reference to the functional advantages of these arrangements, while also giving an account of the physical causes involved. Democritus (about 460–370 BC), a hard-headed materialist, is criticised for denying purpose in nature and reducing everything to mere necessity.

To speak just of the necessary causes is as if one supposed that the only reason why water had been drawn off dropsical patients was the lancet, and not the patients' health – for the sake of which the lancet made the incisions. (*On the Generation of Animals* V.8.789b12)

Finally, a famous passage in which, near the beginning of his great series of biological lecture-courses, Aristotle encourages the student to recognise the compensations and attractions of this branch of science. No doubt the eternal heavenly bodies are the noblest objects of knowledge, but knowledge about them is hard to come by. We are in a much better position to get information about living things here on earth, and studying them has its own appeal.

It now remains to speak of animals and their nature. We shall try to omit nothing, however mean or lowly. For even in the study of animals that are unattractive to the senses, the nature that fashioned them offers immeasurable pleasures to those who can discover causes and reasons [*aitiai*] and are true lovers of wisdom. After all, we enjoy studying the likenesses of animals because we are at the same time studying the skill (of the painter or sculptor) that fashioned them. How unreasonable and absurd it would be not to delight still more in studying the actual works of nature, provided that we can discern their causes. So we must not approach the examination of the lower animals with a childish distaste; in all natural things there is something wonderful. There is a story about some people who wanted to meet Heraclitus [fifth century BC]. When they came to visit him they saw him in the kitchen, warming himself at the stove, and they hesitated. But Heraclitus said, 'Don't be afraid to come in. There are gods even here.' In the same way, we ought to approach our enquiries about each kind of animal without any aversion, knowing that in every one of them there is something natural and beautiful. For in the works of nature orderliness and purpose are to be found in the highest degree, and the end for the sake of which they have been composed and have come into being is itself a kind of beauty.

Anyone who does think that the study of animals is a mean or unworthy pursuit ought to take the same view about himself. After all, no one can look without a good deal of distaste at the constituents of the human body – blood, flesh, bones, blood-vessels and the like.

In any discussion of parts or pieces of equipment we must not think that it is the material that is the real object of enquiry, but rather the structure as a whole: the house, for example, not the bricks, mortar and timber. In the same way, we must recognise that a student of nature is concerned with the composition and the being as a whole, not with parts that can never exist in separation from the being they belong to. (*Parts of Animals* I.5.645a5)

Comments

The above passages have given an idea of how Aristotle applies his principles of scientific explanation in the field of biology. He aims at providing a teleological explanation in terms of the *good* which some organ or process brings to the animal or plant, and also a non-teleological explanation in terms of the *necessary* materials and movements which bring about those organs or processes. He is right to distinguish these two types of account, and he is right to be interested in both of them. A medical student today will learn about the processes which, in accordance with laws of biochemistry, produce this or that organ in the body, and he will also learn about the contribution to the proper functioning of the body which that organ makes. However, Aristotle's teleological convictions go rather further than this, or at least they seem to do so. For he holds that just as a carpenter's movements are *for the sake of* the object he is making, and are explained by reference to it, so the natural movements that terminate in there being this or that organ, this or that animal, are for the sake of that organ or animal, and so can be properly and primarily explained only by reference to their 'end'. But to say that certain natural processes are for the sake of the organ they produce is more than to say that they do in fact produce the organ, which then serves to help the organism to survive. Aristotle holds that it is not by chance or necessity but by design that nature produces its beneficial effects; they are not just the happy outcome of physico-chemical processes – they are what these processes are *for*, and they explain the occurrence of these processes.

Philosophers of science still argue about teleological explanation – how exactly it is to be analysed, and whether or not it plays an indispensable role in biology.

A few final comments. First a point about *necessity*. Aristotle insists that though there must be iron if there is to be an axe it is not the case that if there is iron there must be an axe; and that the necessity the scientist studies is therefore 'hypothetical necessity'. However, to say that there must be iron if there is to be an axe (that is, a tool capable of chopping down trees) does imply that iron has a certain fixed character and certain fixed powers. Having these it necessarily acts and reacts in definite and predictable ways. This is not necessity of a merely hypothetical kind. An appeal to *hypothetical* necessity, in short, presupposes the recognition of some *absolute* necessity. It might of course be suggested that the existence of iron is in its turn to be explained teleologically: *if* there was to be iron – a useful and 'good' compound – there had to occur such-and-such processes involving the four basic elements. However, this line of thought presupposes that the elements themselves have absolutely fixed and necessary characters. So at least some of the scientist's investigations will be concerned to discover *un*conditional necessities.

Teleology and artefacts   To explain an axe's being made we need to mention not only the material, with its fixed and necessary character, but also what sounds like a quite different and decidedly teleological factor, the skilled craftsman, with a desire for an axe. His goal, what he aims at, controls and explains the materials he chooses and the processes he carries out. But now suppose that we could give a physical or physiological account of the craftsman's skill and of his desire (perhaps as being brain-states). We should then be in a position to state not merely some material conditions necessary for an axe's being produced, but a set, no doubt a very complex set, of material conditions – there being iron etc., and such-and-such brain-states and muscular conditions – which would, taken all together, be *sufficient* for an axe's being produced. This whole set of material conditions would guarantee the production of an axe, in accordance with non-teleological laws. This would surely be a complete explanation of the whole business, leaving no room for an additional or alternative explanation in teleological terms? Or would it still be possible and important to provide, as well, the account of axe-making that used, not the terminology of physics and chemistry, but such terms as 'purpose', 'aim', and 'good'?

Teleology and natural organisms   Special problems about teleology arise when we move from artefacts to natural organisms. It is easy to say not only what the function and purpose of each part of an axe is, but also what the function and purpose of the axe as a whole is. Before the craftsman set out to design and make an axe, he knew exactly what he wanted to do with it, the 'good' he was seeking to bring about. Now with an animal we can certainly explain how some organ serves to keep it alive, given the environment in which it lives and the other kinds of animal it has to contend with. Given such facts, it is useful to the elephant to have a trunk, and we can explain the purposes it serves in the elephant's life. But can we say what the function and purpose of the elephant as a whole is? A part 'serves a purpose' in helping the animal to survive; but what purpose is served by the existence and survival of the animal itself? What is the elephant *for*? What are rats *for*? It used to be suggested that all other animals, as well as plants, are there for the benefit of man – leaving to be answered only the question why God made man. A modern idea would be that particular species of animal play a role in the wider ecological system. Rats keep down some other species which would, if uncontrolled, take over; they help maintain the 'balance of nature'. But then why should these particular species exist at all, and why is this particular balance of nature a good one? Similar questions await Aristotle. He holds that the function of an elephant is to produce another elephant: it is the survival of the species, not of the individual, that is nature's end. But what good is served by the existence of the elephant species, and by the existence of the other species there are? Are they in any way better than other species that there might have been? If not, we may be able to see how natural processes work for the preservation of the universal *status quo*, but we shall hardly be entitled to say that nature works for the good, that it produces the best of all possible worlds.

Aristotle's teleology   This has been interpreted in radically different ways at different times. He has been credited with the (poetical or mystical) notion that Nature has aims and purposes exactly as a craftsman does, that acorns really want and try to become oaks. At the opposite (hard-headed) extreme, it has been held that Aristotle's is an 'as if' teleology: we are not to think that natural organisms actually aim at anything or that natural processes are really for the sake of anything – this is nothing but an anthropomorphic way of speaking, a mere *façon de parler*. This suggestion hardly does justice to the importance Aristotle attaches to teleological explanation in nature, or to the way in which his teleology is finally tied to his theology (pages 133–4). Moreover it leaves a crucial question to be answered: What is it about natural organisms and systems that *tempts* us to speak as if they were teleological systems? On a third interpretation, the foundation of Aristotle's teleology is his belief that the behaviour of plants and animals is incapable of being predicted simply from a knowledge of the material elements and compounds that make them up. He believes that at various stages of complexity and development there are 'jumps', there arrive on the scene 'emergent' properties and powers, whose arrival could not have been foreseen before the development occurred. Biological laws and facts are not, on this view, *reducible* to laws and facts of chemistry and physics; from these last you could not, even in principle, deduce how *living* things would perform. That there are such jumps in nature does not prove that the simpler processes and things are for the sake of the more complex. However, the idea that the more complex, having extra powers, is superior and better is plausible enough. (We too when we speak of 'higher' animals are blending a purely descriptive with a decidedly evaluative thought.) Yet another approach to Aristotle's teleology concentrates on the idea of different language-levels, each of which may employ concepts of its own, not capable of expression at other levels. This idea can be combined with the previous suggestion. For if there *are* properties distinctive of living organisms and not deducible from facts about their material constituents, the (biological) language that speaks of such properties will be at a different level and will employ different concepts from the (physico-chemical) language that can state only the facts about the constituents. Something more will be said about this towards the end of the next chapter.

5 The philosophy of mind

Recent years have seen much lively work on the philosophy of mind. This has included general theories about the nature of the mind and its relation to the body, and also analyses of particular psychological activities and concepts such as desire, perception and thought. In nearly every area, what Aristotle had to say, in his brief but highly influential treatises, still interests and stimulates philosophers. Since, as usual, he is working at problems and not offering neatly packaged solutions, there are various tendencies and strands in his work which do not all point in the same direction. So here, as elsewhere, Aristotle is fascinating and important not so much because he supplies the right answers, but because he diagnoses fundamental problems so well, and discusses them with a unique combination of simplicity and subtlety. What he says is often difficult and sometimes unclear, but it is always thought-provoking; the closer one gets to any of his remarks or arguments, the more one finds it to be of philosophical interest.

In this chapter I hope to give an idea of a few main issues in Aristotle's philosophy of mind, and also to convey some impression of the wide range of topics he discusses. I will first outline the general position Aristotle adopts in opposition to the views of his predecessors, and I will give some quotations from the first book of his work 'on the soul' (*De anima*) to illustrate his position. Next, discussion of his account of sense-perception will serve as an example of his treatment of particular psychological faculties. Finally, I will examine his own theory of the soul and its relation to the body.

Aristotle's approach to the mind–body problem

From very early on the Greeks drew some sort of distinction between a man's body and his soul, his *psyche*. By Aristotle's time this distinction, and the concept of the soul, had developed in such a way that the problems he faced were not greatly different from those faced by a modern philosopher when he tackles the 'mind–body problem' and asks how the mind is related to the body, and how its various powers and activities are related to one another and to bodily events and states. But it is essential to realise that the word *psyche* has a wider meaning than 'mind': to have *psyche* is simply to have life. So all living things, including plants, have soul, are 'ensouled'; they are animate, not inanimate (Latin *anima* = Greek *psyche*). But living things do not all have the same kind of life, the same *psyche*. Plant life is just growing, taking in nutrition, and producing seeds of new plants: plants have only 'vegetative soul'. For animals life is a matter also of sense-perception, of desire and of movement; and men possess in addition the faculty of thought. Aristotle was a biologist, and he saw life as a sort of continuum from the lowest or simplest to the highest and most complex of living things. He was not at all inclined to think of the soul as a supernatural indwelling substance. This is a view that can be very tempting if one regards thought or consciousness as essential to the soul; it is not nearly so tempting to one who recognises plants too as being alive, and therefore as having souls.

In his psychological investigations Aristotle keeps the physical aspect of psychological activites very much to the fore. He rejects the dualism of soul and body which he found in Plato as firmly as modern philosophers have come to reject the dualism of René Descartes (1596–1650). A person – or a dog – is not one thing inside another, a spirit imprisoned in a body or a 'ghost in a machine', but a special kind of complex unity. Nor are his soul and his body *parts* of a person or of an animal (any more than its shape and its timber are parts of a table). We must not think that it is Tom's *soul* that feels thirst and desires water, while it is his *body* that runs to the stream. It is *Tom* who feels thirst and desires water, and it is *Tom* who runs to the stream. It may well be useful to classify certain facts about Tom as psychological facts and other facts as physical facts; but this does not mean that the two sets of facts are about different things. They can be about one and the same thing considered in different ways, under different aspects. (Remember the man who lost his job as cook but was re-elected chairman.) I may describe and criticise the performance of a symphony from a purely technical point of view or again from a purely aesthetic or artistic point of view; this does not mean that the two accounts are about different performances.

There are several ways in which physical facts may be connected with psychological activities. Consider an emotion, say anger. Feelings, thoughts and the desire for retaliation are certainly ingredients in anger. There are also various kinds of physical aspect. There is the behaviour of the angry person, what he *does* because he is angry: he throws a brick through the window. There are other visible bodily signs of his emotion, not things he does but things that happen to him: he goes red, and the veins on his neck swell. And there are *inner* physiological changes and processes that are not easily, if at all, observable: changes in the chemical composition of the blood, electrical impulses in the nervous system. What then really *is* anger? How do the various physical goings-on enter into the account? Take, for example, the inner physiological changes. Are they the cause of anger, or the effect of anger, or are they a part of anger itself? Or are they, even, all that anger really is: is anger really *nothing but* a condition of certain parts of the body? Now Aristotle was of course not well-informed about the actual physiological processes involved in anger. But this does not prevent him from having the same fundamental philosophical problem as we do. To the scientist it is a question of primary importance whether it is in the heart or in the brain that certain distinctive changes occur when a person is angry; to the philosopher this question is almost a matter of indifference. When Aristotle offers an account of the physiology of emotion or perception or memory he does certainly hope to be giving the correct account, and he appeals to empirical evidence where available – he is, after all, as we should say, a scientist as well as a philosopher. But he often recognises the grave limitations on his knowledge in this area – many questions await further observations and evidence; and he often remarks that for theoretical puzzles the factual details are irrelevant. So, for instance, philosophical problems about the unity of the self and the relation of mind to body are not affected by whether it is the heart or the brain that receives signals from the sense-organs and sends signals to the hands and legs. To return to anger, the philosopher's questions are such as these: if there is some physical process p that always occurs in a person's body when he is angry, is his being angry *identical* with the occurrence of p? If it is not identical, how is it related to the occurrence of p? Is anger a strictly mental state – the desire for retaliation – which causes p, or is caused by p; or does anger somehow include p?

Consider now that most fundamental animal faculty, sense-perception. An essential element in every episode of perceiving is that there is something 'out there' which causes (or anyway is causally connected with) the perceiver's experience. If there is nothing really there, we do not count it as a case of perception. In this respect sense-perception differs from anger. Anger certainly involves the *belief* that someone out there has actually done something offensive. But I can be really angry with someone for doing something, though I am in fact mistaken in thinking that he did it. With perception things are different: I cannot be really seeing or touching a cat if in fact there is no cat there; I only think I see a cat, I only seem to be touching a cat. Clearly, therefore, a proper account of sense-perception will have to mention environmental factors in addition to facts about the perceiver's sensations and physiology, and it will have to say something about the causal connection there must be between the perceived thing and the perceiver. As with anger, however, it is one thing to recognise that there must be such a causal connection, and another thing to be able to give a correct scientific account of it; and the philosophical questions arise equally whether one can or cannot give such an account. There must be eyes and internal physiological processes if there is to be seeing, and there must also be external objects causing changes in eyes. But does seeing *consist* in these physical and physiological processes? Or is it an event that occurs at the end of all these processes, perhaps an act of awareness? But if *this* is what seeing is, it *might* presumably occur even in the absence of the usual preceding processes – in which case sight would not by definition require that any such processes had occurred. If, however, seeing consists in the processes *plus* an act of awareness, how are the processes and the act related? Here again, what is archaic and obsolete in Aristotle's account of the physics of sense-perception, as of its physiology, need not affect the interest and value of his philosophising about the problems of perception.

To put the main issue in the most general terms, what is the relation or connection between psychological events, processes or states, and physical or physiological events, processes or states? Modern physics and physiology have achieved an entirely new understanding of the brain and the nervous system. But if philosophy has a better answer to the mind–body problem than the Greeks, it is not because of such scientific advances, but because of increased refinement and subtlety in the conceptual analysis the problem calls for. It is by no means certain that we do in fact have a better answer: there is no agreement on what the right answer may be, and the rival answers on offer are already to be found, in essential outline, in Greek philosophy.

I do not want to exaggerate the extent to which Aristotle's preoccupations coincide with ours. Some questions now pose themselves because fantastic advances in medical knowledge and technique make us ready to entertain seriously possibilities which would before have seemed too bizarre to think about. We can take seriously the idea of a brain-transplant or of brain-fission, and so we are led to ask what the consequences would be for the identity of the person(s) affected. If A's body were given B's brain, and B's body received A's brain, which of the two people who left the hospital would be A and which would be B? Again, if A's brain were split, one side going into one body and the other side into another body, which of the two resulting people would be A – or would A now be two people? We may hope that Aristotle's general theory of soul and body will suggest a way of dealing with such questions, but it would be absurd to expect him to discuss them explicitly. (He does in fact make a few remarks which come quite close to these issues. His comments on the controlling role of the heart as the 'seat of life' anticipate the idea that the brain is the bearer of personal identity – so that in the transplant example it is the body with A's brain that would be A. His allusion to the independent survival of the two worm-parts when a worm is cut in two raises a problem not unlike that of brain-fission.)

Certain other problems much discussed in modern philosophy are due to the idea that mental life is *private*. If feelings, desires, perceptions and thoughts are essentially private events of which only their owner can be directly aware, how can I know – or even have the least reason to believe – that others have a mind at all? And, supposing that they do have minds, how can I know what is going on in them? What possible reason can I have to believe that when you shout and go red you are feeling a private anger-feeling like the one I feel on similar occasions? Such scepticism about the existence of other minds, and sceptical questions about our knowledge of other people's thoughts and feelings, do not worry Aristotle. He takes for granted (here as elsewhere) what we all cannot help taking for granted; he does not try to prove or justify the obvious. It may be thought a large gap in his philosophy of mind that he does not pay serious attention to phenomena such as concealment and deception, the keeping hidden of one's thoughts and feelings. On the other hand his lack of interest in these aspects of privacy saved him from some rather barren perplexities. Concealment and deceit are necessarily abnormal, and capable of being explained and understood only as deviations from the normal; and so it is important that the theorist should first and foremost concentrate on and explain the ordinary, straightforward operations of the mind.

Some illustrative texts

A few passages from the first book of the *De anima* will illustrate some of the points just made. This book is mainly concerned with criticism of Aristotle's predecessors and especially of dualism – the idea of the soul as some kind of indwelling *thing* ('substance'). Aristotle insists that the psychological faculties, with only one special exception, are powers *of* and *in* bodies, and that it is the 'ensouled' (i.e. living) body – the man or the animal or the plant – that feeds, perceives, desires, moves. To speak of the soul is to speak of 'something about' a plant or an animal, of an animal or of a plant qua living, not of some *thing in* a plant or an animal.

There is a problem about the affections of the soul: do they all belong to what *has* the soul, or are there any which belong just to the soul itself? Not an easy question, but it must be answered. In most cases it seems that the soul is not affected without the body, and does nothing without it – for example, being angry, feeling confident, desiring, and perceiving in general. What most seems to belong just to the soul is thinking [since no bodily processes are obviously involved in think-ing]; but if thinking either is a sort of imagination or is impossible without imagination, then it too could not possibly occur without the body [since imagination depends on previous sense-perception, and sense-perception involves the body].

Now if there is anything the soul does or undergoes which belongs just to it, the soul would be capable of being separated from the body. If there is no such thing, it could not exist in separation, but it will be like what is straight, which has many properties *in virtue of* its being straight [qua straight], e.g. touching a bronze sphere at a point, though its *being straight* cannot itself touch anything in this way: straightness cannot exist in separation, since it is always with some body. [What a straight ruler can do qua straight is like what a living body can do qua living. Neither the straightness of the ruler nor the life of the plant or animal is a separate thing.] All the affections of the soul are also, it seems, with a body – anger, calm, fear, pity, confidence, joy, loving and hating: together with these the body is affected in some way. Witness the fact that sometimes strong and vivid impressions occur without our being aroused or feeling afraid, while at other times we are moved by weak and feeble impressions – that is, at times when the body is in a state of excitement, similar to its state when one is angry. Even when absolutely nothing frightening is occurring people can find themselves with the feelings of one who is frightened. (*De anima* I.1.403a3)

In view of this involvement of the body in the 'affections of the soul' the psychologist will have to give what we should call a psychophysical account of the activities and faculties which he investigates, just as we saw before that the student of nature in general must concern himself with both form and matter.

Their definitions must therefore be of this kind: being angry is a certain change of such and such a body (or part or faculty of a body) caused by this or that and for this or that. A scientist would define an affection of soul differently from a dialectician: the latter would define anger as a desire for retaliation, or something of the sort, while the former might define it as a boiling of the blood and hot stuff around the heart. One of them is giving the matter, the other the form and essential account [*logos*] – for his is the essential account of the thing, though it must be in a certain kind of matter if it is to exist. Thus the essential account of a house is (say) that it is a shelter against destruction by wind, rain and heat. One man may describe it as stones, bricks and timbers, while another will say that it is the form in them for the sake of such-and-such. [The latter will define it as a certain sort of *structure* designed to serve a certain *purpose*.] Which then of these is the natural scientist? The one concerned with matter and ignorant of the essential account, or the one concerned only with the essential account? Is it not rather the one who combines both? (*De anima* I.1.403a25)

Aristotle criticises the cavalier way in which philosophers speak of souls as being in bodies, without taking account of the fact that the various powers and activities of the soul – of life – need appropriate bodily organs. A given form of life demands a certain definite kind of body. You can't exercise skill at typewriting unless you have a typewriter, and the power of sight can be exercised only with the aid of eyes.

There is something odd about most theories of the soul. They attach the soul to the body – put it into the body – but do not explain why it is in a body, nor do they say what condition the body has to be in. Yet this is surely necessary. For because of their association the one acts and the other is acted upon, and the one is moved by the other; and this sort of interaction does not take place between any two random things whatsoever. But they only undertake to say what sort of thing the soul is, and they add no account of the body that is to receive it – as if it were possible (as in the Pythagorean stories) for any soul whatsoever to enter into any any body whatsoever. In fact, each body seems to have its own peculiar form and shape. One might just as well speak of skill at carpentry entering into flutes: a skill has to use its tools – and a soul has to use its body. (*De anima* I.3.407b13)

We do often speak *as if* the soul were a kind of thing which itself undergoes changes and does things. Really, however, it is the person or the animal – the living body – that undergoes changes and does things.

We say that the soul is grieved or pleased, is confident or afraid, or is angry or perceives or thinks. All these seem to be changes, and it might be inferred that the soul itself is changed. But this is not necessarily so. We may allow that being grieved or being pleased or thinking are changes, and that the change is due to the soul. (We may suppose, for example, that being angry or afraid is the heart's being changed in a certain way, and that thinking too is a change in this or some other part – the details of the changes are not at present relevant.) Yet to say that it is the soul that is angry is as if one were to say that it is the soul that weaves or builds. It is surely better not to say that the *soul* pities or learns or thinks, but rather that the *man* does this *with* his soul. It is not that the change is in the soul, but that sometimes it reaches as far as the soul, and sometimes it starts from it. Perception, for example, comes *from* certain objects *to* the soul, whereas recollection starts *from* the soul and extends *to* movements or traces in the sense-organs. (*De anima* I.4.408b1)

In the above two extracts Aristotle has said that a soul *uses* its body, and that a man does certain things *with* his soul. Both these remarks need interpretation. The soul does not use the body as a craftsman uses tools, but rather as a craft (such as skill at carpentry) may be said to use tools, in that it is necessarily exercised and displayed through the movement of tools. The powers distinctive of living things are exercised and displayed in the movements of their bodies. And just as tools are for the sake of the craft or skill, and not vice versa, so bodily organs are for the sake of their functions, not vice versa: eyes are for seeing. The other phrase, 'a man does things with his soul', is also not analogous to 'a craftsman does things with his tools', but rather to 'a craftsman does things with his skill'. It is in virtue of his being alive, having faculties of nutrition and desire, that an animal feeds and desires; in other words, the animal feeds and desires 'with his soul'.

That anger and sense-perception have physical aspects is rather obvious. What about thought? Aristotle believes that ordinary everyday thinking involves the use of images, which are themselves psychophysical phenomena; and that such thinking is therefore 'common' to soul and body. He does, however, admit the possibility of pure thought, of an intellect (*nous*) which can grasp pure forms immediately and without the aid of imagery. Such an intellect, he holds, *could* be 'separable' from body altogether.

This claim may be taken in either of two ways. It may be understood simply as the claim that a man could think of abstract topics without undergoing any associated bodily changes. It may be taken as the much stronger claim that such thought could occur without the thinker's having a body at all; and this seems to be what Aristotle intends. The idea of a pure intellect literally separable from the body is difficult to understand, and difficult to reconcile with the rest of Aristotle's philosophy of mind. It is to be found not only in the *De anima* but also in the *Metaphysics* (where, as we shall see, God is identified as pure thought), and in the treatise on the generation of animals:

Principles whose activity is bodily clearly cannot be present without a body, just as one cannot walk without feet. So they [such faculties as

those of nutrition and perception] cannot enter the body from outside
. . . they cannot exist separately . . . It remains that only intellect [*nous*]
enters from outside and only intellect is divine. For *its* activity is not
associated with any bodily activity. (*De generatione animalium*
II.3.736b22)

Sense-perception and other faculties

We shall return to the general mind–body problem in the next section,
and shall consider the definition of the soul which Aristotle gives at the
beginning of *De anima* II. But it will be useful first to outline some of his
ideas about particular psychological powers and about their interconnec-
tions.

Plants exhibit the lowest and simplest form of life; they possess just the
'vegetative soul'. They can take in nutriment, grow, and produce seeds
from which new plants develop. Animals too have nutritive and genera-
tive powers, but they are distinguished from plants by having sense-
perception also. With sense-perception come imagination (decayed perception), desire (stimulated by perception or imagination) and movement
(caused by desire). These faculties are connected with one another, and
the connection is conceptual. You could not, for example, explain what
desire *is* without bringing in the idea of an *object* of desire, something
perceived or at least envisaged, and also the idea of *going after* that object.
Aristotle puts this point very strongly: 'desire – active desire – is the same
as pursuit [or avoidance], and the faculties of desire and of pursuit [or
avoidance] are not different from one another or from the faculty of
perception. But their *being* is not the same [on this phrase see pages 9 and 38].'
The faculties in question are not actually separable from one another, but
only distinguishable in thought. To speak of, say, desire is to speak of
one aspect of a total situation which necessarily contains other aspects:
the identifying by perception or in the imagination of an object of desire,
and the tendency to go after it.

Besides this conceptual connection between the animal faculties there
is a teleological connection which Aristotle often emphasises. Not only
couldn't there be desire without perception to provide an object of desire,
but also there would be no *point* in having the power of perception unless
one had also the power of desire. And desire in turn would be pointless if
the animal could not go after what it desired. All these faculties work
together to enable the animal to survive in a dangerous world, to react to
its environment, seeking out the food that preserves it (and which it finds
pleasant) and avoiding what harms and hurts it. It would be useless, and
therefore unnatural, for a creature to be able to recognise imminent

danger if it had no means of avoiding it; and pointless to have the means of moving about without the ability to distinguish features in the environment. Here is a short passage that illustrates Aristotle's approach.

> An animal must have sense-perception, and there can be no animal without this faculty, if nature does nothing pointless. For everything that exists by nature is *for* something (or will be found to be an accidental concomitant of things that *are* for something). Now any body capable of walking would, if it lacked perception, be destroyed and fail to attain its end, which is its natural job. For how could it feed itself? It follows that no body which has soul is able to move but unable to perceive. (*De anima* III.12.434a30)

Here is a passage, from Aristotle's monograph on sense-perception, which makes some points about the role of the different particular senses and their relations to one another.

> Turning to the various particular senses, touch and taste necessarily belong to all animals, touch for the reason given in *De anima* ['since an animal is a living body, and every body is tangible, the body of an animal must have the sense of touch, if the animal is to survive ... Unless it has the sense of touch it will not be able, when it is touched, to avoid some things and take others'], and taste because of nutrition. For it is by taste that an animal discriminates what is pleasant and unpleasant in food, so as to avoid the one and go after the other.
>
> The senses that operate through external media – smell, hearing and sight – belong to animals which can move. In all of them the senses are for their preservation – in order that the animals may perceive in advance the food to go after and the bad and destructive things to avoid; but in those that have intelligence as well the senses are [not simply for their being, but also] for their *well*-being. The senses inform them of many distinctions, and from these both theoretical and practical intelligence develop.
>
> Of the senses sight is in itself superior as regards the necessities of life, but for knowledge hearing is incidentally superior. Many and various are the distinctions reported by the faculty of sight, because all bodies are coloured – so that the 'common sensibles' (shape, size, movement, number) are also perceived mainly through this sense; whereas hearing reports only distinctions of sound, and also to a few animals those of voice. Incidentally, however, hearing contributes most to intelligence, since speech, which is audible, is responsible for learning – not in itself, but incidentally: it is composed of words, and each word is a symbol. That is why among those who lack one or other

sense from birth the blind are more intelligent than the deaf and dumb. (*De sensu* 1.436b12)

Just as an animal's powers of perception etc. affect its nutritive and procreative activities, introducing possibilities and complexities of which plants are incapable, so man's power of thought profoundly influences the way in which perception and desire work in him. He can articulate and describe what he perceives, he can formulate and communicate long-range desires and work out ways to satisfy them, he can develop social arrangements and institutions that depend on rules and ideas intelligible only to language-users. So he is in a better position to deal with his environment and to survive, while his form of life is also more varied, richer, 'higher' than that of living things which lack the power of thought.

Perception can no doubt be enjoyed for its own sake, even where no practical question is involved. Still more so with thought. The desire to know far outstrips the desire to know what is or may be of practical importance. Here, with 'theoretical' thought and the knowledge it achieves, we reach the highest activity a living thing is capable of – and an activity that no longer seems to require or involve bodily processes and needs.

It will not be possible to examine Aristotle's discussions of all the powers and activities of living things. By way of a sample I will indicate the main lines of his theory of perception. I hope to say enough to give the flavour of Aristotle's treatment, and to show how close it comes to some modern preoccupations. Here is a short passage that sums up his view that perceiving is 'receiving the form without the matter', and also contains a striking comment on the relation of bodily organs to psychological faculties.

As for sense-perception in general, it must be understood that the faculty of perception is the capacity to receive perceptible forms without matter, as wax receives the ring's seal-engraving without its iron or gold: it takes the golden or bronze engraving, but not qua gold or bronze. Similarly, the perception of anything is affected by what has colour or taste or sound, but not in so far as it is called that particular thing, but only in so far as it is qualified in such-and-such a way, i.e. in virtue of its character.

The primary sense-organ is that in which the above power resides. It is in fact the same [as the power], though its being [what it is] is different. For what perceives must be a certain magnitude, whereas the capacity to perceive, the faculty of perception, is obviously not a magnitude, but a sort of essential character, the organ's power. (*De anima* II.12.424a17)

What can Aristotle mean when he says that the faculty of perception is the power to receive form without matter? He is certainly not suggesting that sense-perception is a kind of telepathy, since he always insists that physical and physiological processes are essential to it. Yet his point can hardly be that when I see an apple no bit of apple enters my eye. If that were the crucial point one would have to grant that mirrors see apples, since a mirror certainly takes on characteristics of the apple it reflects, without any bit of apple entering it. Perhaps Aristotle's view is that perceiving something is being aware of it, awareness being a non-physical event that occurs at the end of a chain of physical and physiological processes. But there is not much direct evidence for this interpretation. To get closer to Aristotle's meaning, let us briefly consider his account of the processes and purposes of perception.

Aristotle supposes that changes of some kind are conveyed to our sense-organs through a medium – air or water in the case of sight and hearing and smell; and that they are then passed on to the centre, 'whether heart or brain makes no difference'. This centre is itself strictly speaking the primary sense-organ. (That seeing is not just a matter of the eye's functioning properly is shown by the fact that damage behind the eye can deprive a person of the power of sight.) The exact nature of the changes that Aristotle supposes to occur is not clear. His fullest discussion is in connection with sight, but his account of the transmission of colour from the external object to the eye is very difficult to understand. The changes *inside* the body are sometimes spoken of as if they were movements of blood, sometimes as if they were movements carried in the blood, and sometimes as if they were qualitative changes. The real facts are no doubt beyond Aristotle's ken. The two crucial points he is making are that in sense-perception there must be a physical and physiological causal chain from object to primary sense-organ, and that the change at the end of the chain must be like, or in some way correspond to, the changes at earlier stages and at the beginning. This second requirement is obviously intended to help explain why the outcome of the processes involved in seeing a blue triangle should be the seeing of a *blue triangle*. It is a requirement that may be construed crudely or may be given quite a sophisticated interpretation. This will depend on what *kind* of likeness or correspondence is supposed to be necessary. Electrical impulses carried over a telephone wire are not much like the audible sounds they convey, but such impulses do correspond to sounds in a certain way. Again, coded messages and translations may not look at all like their originals, but they can carry the same content. A sequence of dots and dashes in morse says the same as a sentence in English, and various bits of the sequence correspond to various bits of the sentence. The idea is now familiar that in sense-perception the changes that go through the nervous system to the brain convey in a sort of coded form the characteristics of perceived objects, messages which the brain decodes. This may be regarded as a refined version of Aristotle's account.

To explain imagination, memory and dreams, Aristotle supposes that the movements that reach the heart in sense-perception persist in that region. They are physical traces which usually remain submerged, ineffective, unnoticed, but which under suitable circumstances get reactivated (or come to the surface, to use an Aristotelian metaphor); then they appear to us as images. It will depend on other factors – the nature of the stimulus, the condition and beliefs of the person – whether the having of such an image is (also) a case of memory or of dreaming. The key point is that imagination and memory cannot be explained without some assumptions about physical traces. Exactly what these may be like (electrical? chemical?) and where they may be (in the heart or in the brain), are important but secondary questions. For the philosopher the first and essential thing is that there must be *some* such traces, capable of reactivation. For this much is implied in the very concepts of imagination and of memory, even though the actual processes of storage and retrieval may be quite unknown to us.

If an animal is to react discriminatingly to its environment, moving to get food and to avoid harm (the point and purpose of sense-perception), information about its environment must be conveyed to a unitary centre which can receive and coordinate the input from different senses, and which can initiate the necessary reactive movements. Aristotle argues persuasively that the very notion of an animal – a single, self-contained, mobile organism – requires there to be such a single centre (which he thinks to be the heart) at which all perceptual chains terminate and all reactive chains begin. He is not suggesting, of course, that it is the heart that perceives the apple or is attracted by it. The animal is the percipient – but this is so *because* it possesses a heart and the complex physiological make-up needed for the heart to function, receiving information from the environment and initiating movements by the animal.

The characters of external objects are conveyed by physical and physiological processes to a centre in the animal body from which reactive movements begin, movements directed to securing what is beneficial and avoiding what is harmful to the animal. This is certainly a large part of Aristotle's view of sense-perception, and we can easily see why he would not say that a mirror perceives the apple it reflects, or even that a magnet perceives the iron filings it attracts. Can we also derive from the view outlined above a clue to the interpretation of his statement that perceiving is receiving form without matter? The movement that reaches the heart in perception carries the character (form) of the external thing, not the thing itself. The character is received in that it arrives at a centre from which begin reactions that are to be explained as movements to take or to avoid the thing because of that character. One might say that an animal *takes in* the characteristics of its environment; for it reacts to them in ways we can understand teleologically, almost as if it had intelligence and could understand what would be good for it. A mirror does *not* (in this sense) take in the characteristics it takes on.

Aristotle's thoroughly biological account of perception, and of its necessary connections with desire and movement, lays no stress on private acts of awareness. To anyone who thinks that such acts of consciousness are the very essence of sense-perception Aristotle's account must seem laughably inadequate. If, however, one recognises that animals, even very lowly animals, can perceive, his explanation may seem to capture what is essential. He should not be seen as turning animals into mere machines just because he does not attribute to them private acts of awareness. It is their complex powers that distinguish animals from machines – and make them wonderful – not the occurrence in them of private mental acts. Not that Aristotle's account need rule out acts of awareness. He could perfectly well allow that in the case of men (and some other 'higher' animals) the processes that constitute basic sense-perception are enriched by a further process that constitutes awareness of the basic sense-perception.

In the second paragraph of the passage I quoted above Aristotle *identifies* the primary sense-organ with the faculty of perception, that is, with the 'perceptive soul'. How can a bodily organ (or more generally the body) be *identical* with the perceptive soul (or more generally the soul)? Aristotle grants that 'their *being* is different': being the body is not the same as being the soul, even though it is one and the same thing that is body and soul. This dark saying leads into the topic of the next section.

Aristotle's account of the soul

In this section I give a translation of the first chapter of *De anima* II. The very general account of the soul that Aristotle gives here is difficult. He makes use in it of ideas developed more fully elsewhere, including the books of *Physics* outlined above. I shall try to help the reader by a fairly free use of interspersed comment.

So much for our predecessors' views about the soul. Let us now dismiss them and make a fresh start. We must try to determine what soul is, what the most general account of it would be.

Now we speak of *substance* [*ousia*] as one type of thing there is, and we speak of substance (i) as matter, that which in itself is not a 'this' [material, not an individual thing of any definite sort; e.g. wood]; and (ii) as shape or form, that in virtue of which a thing is called a 'this' [the shape and structure in virtue of which some material such as wood is a definite thing, such as a table]; and thirdly (iii) as the compound of matter and form [e.g. a wooden table]. Now matter is potentiality, while form is actuality – and that in two ways: (*a*) knowledge is one type of actuality, (*b*) the exercising of knowledge is another. [Timber is only potentially a table; when given shape and structure it is actually a table, though not yet being used as such; when in use it is fully actualising its potential. The child is potentially a mathematician, he is capable of acquiring knowledge; after training he is a mathematician, he possesses knowledge; when he then does mathematics he is exercising knowledge. In both examples the first move is from potentiality to 'first actuality', the second is from first actuality to second actuality.]

Aristotle now applies these ideas to the special case of the living body. The soul is substance in sense (ii), *form*; and it is form or actuality of type (*a*), *first* actuality.

It is above all bodies that are thought to be substances, and especially natural bodies, since they are the principles of the others. Some natural bodies have life, while others do not – by life we mean self-nutrition and growth (and corresponding decay). So every natural body which has life must be a substance, a substance of the composite type [that is, substance in sense (iii) above].

But since it is a body of a certain character – namely, having life – the body cannot itself *be* soul [i.e. life]; the body is not attributed to a subject, but rather serves as subject and matter ['The body has life' is like 'The timber has shape']. The soul must therefore be substance as *the form of a natural body which potentially has life*. But substance is actuality, and thus soul is the actuality of that sort of body. Now we speak of actuality in two ways: knowledge is one type of actuality, the exercising of knowledge is another. The soul is evidently like knowledge. For both sleeping and waking depend on the presence of soul, and waking corresponds to the exercising of knowledge, and sleeping to having knowledge without using it; and in a given individual the knowledge comes first. The soul therefore is *the first actuality of a natural body which potentially has life*.

To say that this body is *alive* is, according to Aristotle, to say that it has powers of a certain kind – those that distinguish living things from others – not that it is at this moment necessarily exercising any of them. It seems rather doubtful whether this is true: an animal asleep or even unconscious is surely exercising *some* living powers – it is, for example, breathing.

Aristotle now asks what kind of natural body does potentially have life, and he suggests that it is one that has organs. Organs are defined by reference to their functions, and natural bodies that have parts so defined are alive.

Any body which has organs is of this kind. Even the parts of plants are organs, though extremely simple ones. For instance, the leaf is a shelter for the pod, the pod for the fruit; and the roots of plants are analogous to the mouth, since both take in food. So if we have to say something applicable to every type of soul, we must say that the soul is *the first actuality of a natural body which has organs*.

In view of this we do not have to enquire whether the soul and the body are one, any more than whether the wax and its shape are one, or in general whether the matter and that whose matter it is are one. For 'one' (like 'is') is used in various ways, but the actuality is what is most strictly one.

To speak of soul, then, is to speak of the ability to do certain things, the things that distinguish the living from the non-living. It is having a certain kind of soul, the nutritive, the perceptive etc., that makes something a plant, or an animal, or a man. Having a soul is precisely what makes this collection of flesh, bones etc. an animal – and *one* animal – just as the shape and structure are what makes some timber *one* thing, namely a table. We must not ask how the shape can be *one with* the timber. The *one thing* is the shaped timber, the table. Form and matter are not identical with one another; rather, the matter is only identifiable as e.g. a table, as possessing form. Matter is made one thing by having such-and-such a form.

Aristotle now proceeds to give further explanation with the aid of analogies.

We have now said in general what the soul is: it is substance as defining essence [*logos*]. And this is the 'what it is to be' of such and such a body. [What is it for some timber to be a table? It is for it to be shaped and put together in a certain way. The shape and structure are the 'essence' and 'what it is to be' of a table.]

Suppose some tool, say an axe, were a natural body. Its essence would be what it is to be an axe, and this would be its soul; if this were taken away it would no longer *be* an axe except in name. (In fact, of course, it is merely an axe. The soul is the 'what it is to be' or essence not of that sort of body, but of a certain kind of *natural* body, one that has in itself a source of change and rest.)

The same applies if you consider bodily parts. Thus, if the eye were an animal, sight would be its soul, since this is the defining essence of an eye. The eye is matter for sight, and if this departs it is no longer an eye except in name, like the eye of a statue or in a painting.

But what is true of a part must be applied to the whole living body. For sense-perception as a whole is related to the whole body which is capable of perception in the same way as a part [a particular sense, like sight] is to a part [a particular sense-organ like the eye].

As cutting and seeing are actualities, so is waking [they are second actualities]; but as sight and the power of the tool are, so is the soul [they are first actualities]; while the body is what potentially is [the body is an animal only in virtue of having soul].

Aristotle now draws his important conclusion. Life (i.e. soul) in its various forms can no more exist apart from living bodies than sight apart from seeing eyes or cutting apart from tools that cut. Unless indeed there is some living power that is not the power of any body – an allusion to *nous* (see page 62).

It is obvious then that the soul is inseparable from the body – or at any rate that some parts of it are, if in fact it has parts. For in some cases the actuality *is* that actuality of the parts themselves. However there is nothing to stop some parts being separable, owing to their being actualities of *no* body.

This must suffice as our outline of the soul.

Aristotle's theory of the soul and its relation to the body is sometimes called 'hylemorphism', from the words *hyle* (matter) and *morphe* (form). Two sorts of question about this theory have been vigorously debated in recent years. First, do some works of Aristotle contain a view about the soul and body that is *different* from the hylemorphic theory; and if so, what are the implications for Aristotle's intellectual development and for the chronology of his writings? Secondly, what is the hylemorphic theory really saying, how is it related to familiar modern answers to the mind–body problem, and what are its strengths and weaknesses? I shall report very briefly the state of play as regards the first question, and then open up some of the issues raised by the second – the strictly philosophical – question.

In a book published in 1948 a Dutch scholar, Fr Nuyens, argued that three different and incompatible theories about the soul can be found in Aristotle, and that we can tell which came first, which second and which third in the development of his thought. The three theories are (i) dualism, the view that the soul and the body are independent substances, each capable of separate existence; (ii) instrumentalism, the view that the body is the soul's instrument, and that the soul (located somewhere in the body) uses the body to carry out its activities; (iii) hylemorphism, the view that the soul is the form, and the body the matter, of the living thing. Nuyens's view is, in outline, as follows. Dualism is to be found in at least one very early work of Aristotle, written when he was still a pupil at Plato's Academy. Dualism was the doctrine of such famous Platonic dialogues as the *Phaedo* and the *Republic*; and in Aristotle it represents his early, Platonising, phase. Hylemorphism, on the other hand, is the latest and most distinctively Aristotelian theory, dominant in works (such as *De anima*) which are already, for other reasons, believed to be late. Instrumentalism is a sort of transitional theory: it treats the soul as more like an independent thing than hylemorphism does, but it connects soul and body more closely than dualism does. So works in which instrumentalism is to be found will have been written after those that contain dualism and before those that contain hylemorphism.

Matters are not as simple as this condensed summary suggests. In the first place, it is often disputable whether a certain phrase or passage does in fact contain or imply one theory rather than another. It is risky to read their full theoretical implications into phrases used casually in the course of discussions about quite other topics. Various ways of speaking about the soul and the body are familiar in ordinary talk, and it is not to be expected that a philosopher would always avoid such ways just because they might, taken literally, suggest a view of the mind and body different from his own official theory. Add the fact that a given work may seem to contain one theory in one place and another theory in another, and it is clear that detecting the three theories and establishing the chronology of works (or parts of works) by reference to the theories contained in them must be a very difficult and delicate task, unlikely to yield clear and generally acceptable results.

Secondly, it is apparent that Aristotle himself did not think that instrumentalist talk *was* incompatible with hylemorphism. For he is prepared to say in one breath that the soul is the form of the body, *and* that the soul is 'in the heart' and 'uses' the body – though the location of the soul in a particular organ and the terminology of 'using' are taken by Nuyens to be decisive evidence of the instrumentalist view. So perhaps hylemorphism, properly understood, is perfectly consistent with the kind of talk characteristic of instrumentalism. Of course, the idea that the soul uses the body seems utterly different from the idea that the soul is the form of the body, if we have in our mind as the standard example of form and matter the shape and the material of, say, a table. The table's shape cannot be said to *use* the wood. Supposing, however, that we identify the form of an artefact – a table or a radio – not with its external shape but with its function, its power to do the job that a table or a radio must (by definition) be able to do. We can now say things that come very close to instrumentalist talk about the soul. The material parts of a table or a radio are there to serve the purpose of the thing, to enable the table to support solid objects or to enable the radio to receive broadcasts; if we ask of any of its parts 'What is the *use* of that?' we get an answer which refers to the job or function of the whole thing.

How then *is* Aristotle's hylemorphism to be understood? Does it solve the mind–body problem? Modern philosophers reject, as Aristotle does, the idea that body and soul are two *things*, and they proceed to argue about the relation between two sets of *events*, psychological or mental events and physiological or physical events. Are bodily events causes, or effects, of mental events? Or are there two independent but perfectly correlated sets of events? Or are mental events actually identical with physical events – is my having a thought just a change in my brain? But if we want to know how Aristotle views these problems, we are frustrated by the fact that he does not state his theory in terms of bodily and mental events, and their interrelation, and that it is not easy to see how the general idea of form and matter (or the parallel idea of actuality and potentiality) can be construed in such a way as to apply to sets of events. Let us return to the table. The distinction between what it is made of (its matter) and its shape or function (its form) is not easily seen as a distinction between two sets of events. No doubt some things are true of the table in virtue of its shape (qua so shaped), certain other things in virtue of its materials (qua wooden): it is combustible because made of wood, it is stable because four-legged. But this distinction does not seem to provide us with two sets of events. Nor indeed does the simple case of the table suggest any immediately plausible interpretation of the thesis that the soul is the form of the body. 'A table is made of wood, with a flat top capable of supporting things' is a long way from 'A person is flesh and bones arranged in a way that enables him to perceive and desire.' For the table's supporting things is just another fact about the material, inanimate world; whereas a person's perceiving things is a fact about the living. The very importance of the distinction between the living and non-living guarantees the difficulty there must be in taking an idea introduced and explained by reference to the non-living, and applying it without further ado to the living.

Nor are we much helped if we turn from Aristotle's highly general and abstract formulae about the soul to his discussion of particular faculties and functions of living things. As regards sense-perception, for example, he gives detailed accounts of physical processes outside and inside the body, and he connects them with our seeing, hearing and so on. But he does not explain how the hylemorphic theory works here. He does not say that seeing etc. are related to physical processes as form to matter, let alone explain what that would mean. It is true that in one important passage about anger (quoted on p. 60 above) he does specify what in this case the form and matter are: desire for retaliation and boiling of the blood. But what it really means to say that the desire is the form and the boiling blood the matter – this remains unclear. Whether desire is thought of as a psychological episode or disposition, or as a tendency to behave in a certain way, the claim that desire and the boiling of the blood make up anger in somewhat the same way as form and matter make a thing is by no means easy to grasp.

Why does Aristotle not see the mind–body problem as a problem about the relationship between two sets of events? One reason perhaps is that he is concerned with *all* living things; animals and plants, as well as men, have *psyche*. He is under no temptation to identify as 'psychological' just those events that involve consciousness and to treat all other events as not involving the soul. But it is particularly if one does concentrate on the private contents of consciousness that one is inclined to draw up a list of events like feeling and sensing and thinking, and a list of public and physical events like breathing and walking and eating. Having drawn up two such lists it is only natural that one should raise queries about how one set of events (the mental) is related to the other (the behavioural or physical). If, on the other hand, your idea of what has soul includes animals and plants (because soul is life), you will of course class breathing, walking and eating along with feeling etc. as psychological. The question will now arise as to exactly how physical and physiological changes of various kinds are related to, say, breathing. But this no longer looks like a question about two radically different sets of events or processes – as though breathing were an event or process quite different from (even if causally connected with) the events or processes going on in nose, throat and lungs. It would be more natural to suggest that breathing just *is* these latter events and processes, but that to describe what goes on as *breathing* is to indicate, in a very general way, the significance of the events and processes in the wider context of the animal's life. Some kind of theory that uses the idea of two levels of description of one and the same set of events seems more appropriate than a theory seeking to relate two quite distinct sets of events.

Let us return to a matter–form compound that seemed to raise no difficulty, the easy example of a table or a house, where the distinction between what it is made of and its shape or structure is clear enough. As we saw, Aristotle soon moves from the idea of form as shape or structure to that of form as the capacity for a job or function: a house is a *shelter* made of such-and-such materials. Now a job or function is something done over a period of time, a capacity actualised in particular perform-ances. So, without yet advancing to the problem of living things, we can ask how the matter–form analysis will work when we consider, say, a house *over a period of time*, when we look at the events and processes that make up its history. Does this history contain certain 'formal' items and certain 'material' items? If so, how are they connected?

A house is essentially a shelter. It is made of bricks etc. put together in a certain way, because only if such materials are so arranged can a shelter be made. Its capacity to give shelter defines the kind of thing it is – makes it a house – and also explains and makes intelligible its being made of bricks etc. so arranged. So things we say about the house's ability to give shelter will surely be about its form, that is, about it qua shelter; whereas things we say about its materials will be about its matter. To say that a house keeps out the snow, or that its porch protects visitors from the wind, is to comment upon its ability to give shelter, the ability which makes it a house and is the reason why it was built; to say that it is made of timber and bricks is to talk of its material – what it is made *of*, not what it is made *for*. Consider now the *history* of our house. The parts perform their functions or fail to do so; they wear out, and need repair. Changes occur in the structure of the materials and in their chemical composition. The roof has been keeping out the rain throughout the winter – though the tiles have been imperceptibly wearing away; the front door has often opened and shut, letting people in and out – but the upper hinge is gradually loosening. The uninstructed householder knows and talks about how the house (and its porch, roof etc.) functions, keeping out the snow etc., or how some defect appears (the roof begins to leak). The expert builder can give a detailed scientific account of the exact physical changes and processes that go on when it functions well and again when some part begins to deteriorate. To put it briefly, there are two accounts that can be given of the history of the house – the 'life' of the house: the householder's and the builder's. Nobody will want to say that the house has two separate histories or lives.

Take as another example a radio. There is a striking difference between the accounts of what goes on when a radio works or when it breaks down that are given by the ordinary user on the one hand and by the technical expert on the other. The two accounts or descriptions differ in type, not just detail; they employ utterly different concepts and serve very different purposes. The scientist's story in a way *explains* the user's story, since we can be brought by it to understand *how* the radio works and why it has been going wrong. But in another way the user's story and terminology is basic, and his point of view is the more important, since it is only to serve his purposes that such things are designed and made at all, and it is therefore only by reference to them that what a radio is can be explained. The user's account reveals the formal and final 'cause' of radios (explanation in terms of 'the good'); the technical story gives the material 'cause' (explanation in terms of 'the necessary').

The general idea, which we may hope to find helpful in interpreting Aristotle's theory of soul and body, is that there can be two levels of description of a single thing's history. The one account may be more general than the other, employing different concepts, grouping events by different rules and with different purposes. As my examples show, the relation of one level to another can often be, or be like, the relation of form to matter – the one being concerned with the functioning of the thing as a whole, the other with detailed physical processes in its various parts. In saying all this we go a little, but only a little, beyond Aristotle's explicit statements. If one combines his original account of form and matter with his analysis of types of explanation (the four causes), and if one also allows for his constant use of the idea that we speak of things 'qua so-and-so', that is, under one aspect or from one point of view, then the foregoing suggestions follow almost inevitably.

Consider now a plant's life. It takes in food, grows, produces flowers and seeds, and dies. That it what it is to be a plant; those are the functions that define plants. It is of course by invisible chemical processes that these functions are performed. They could not be performed without some such changes going on. Such changes exemplify scientific laws which operate everywhere; but in the present context the changes in question serve the purpose of producing and maintaining a plant of a particular kind. There is some analogy with the examples of artefacts discussed above. If we give a broad biological account of the plant's life-cycle and its main functions, we are expounding its form (and the final cause); if we descend to a chemical account of the microscopic processes involved, we are giving the material side of the plant's history.

When we move on and up to the animal, with perception and desire and movement, the analogy weakens. For a movement such as walking it is easy to think that there are two possible accounts related in the way we have been considering. What is, seen at the level of daily life, walking to the post-box, is, given a microscopic scientific description, a sequence of innumerable chemical and physical changes. Qua walking the goings-on form part of a person's history qua a person; qua that sequence of changes they form part of his history qua material body subject to the laws of physics and chemistry. For perception and desire, however, it is more difficult to apply the analogy. The physical and physiological changes that go on when a man sees or remembers or desires do not seem to be related to his seeing, remembering and desiring in the way in which physical and physiological changes are related to his walking. Why not? Perhaps it is because we are assuming that perceiving, desiring and so on are private acts of consciousness (capable perhaps of being the causes or the effects of physical changes, but certainly not themselves physical). If we are prepared to waive that assumption, as we may be if we concentrate on the lower animals, and if we think about biological needs and social contexts, it may after all seem plausible to suggest that perception and desire are concepts we use – like those of breathing and walking – to describe and interpret patterns of overt behaviour and physiological change. With the aid of these concepts we conveniently summarise how animals react to their environment and act upon it. A rat, we say, sees some meat, wants it and tries to get it. To say this is not necessarily to ascribe private mental experiences to the rat, or to claim that anything at all is happening other than ordinary physical and physiological processes. We are simply bringing out a certain intelligible pattern in a very complex sequence of events and processes. In much the same way we may speak of a missile as 'seeing' a target and homing in on it. The reason why we do not ascribe real seeing to the missile is that it lacks other biological powers: missiles do not (yet, fortunately) procreate missiles.

But what about the 'higher' animals, and above all men, who can have feelings without showing them, can conceal their desires, can see and think without making any movement? Here we are obviously not speaking just of noticeable patterns of behaviour or of physical change. One idea is that such cases of feeling, perception and desire – in relatively special and sophisticated situations – are necessarily *secondary* to the plain straightforward cases in which patterns of overt behaviour are being identified and explained. But if this is so, we need to be told how and why this secondary use could have come to be adopted and understood. How could the step be made from talk about ordinary, public episodes involving perception, thought and desire to talk about private, hidden experiences? The question is rather like the one that confronts the psychologist who wants to extend the familiar notion of desire and to speak of *unconscious* desires. He must explain this extended concept and make clear how we are to use it – how we are to identify unconscious desires and decide whether or not an unconscious desire is present in a given person.

In any case, of course, we are faced not only with a linguistic question, as to how a certain secondary use of psychological terms is to be understood, but with an awkward and compelling fact: we are all individually aware of having our own private experiences, often when nobody else suspects it. No talk about patterns of behaviour or secondary uses of words can capture – or conjure out of existence – our private thoughts and feelings. We may allow that to any such experience some physiological event or process corresponds, but the nature of the relationship between the experience and the event or process remains utterly baffling.

Aristotle himself is not worried about puzzles concerning privacy and our knowledge of other minds, any more than he is in general beset by sceptical doubts as to how we can know anything. So a central topic of modern controversy eludes him. There is, however, as we have seen, one very grave difficulty in his overall theory of which he is aware, not the problem of private experience but the problem of pure thought. Supposing that pure thought requires no physical organ or physiological correlate, Aristotle must hold that this kind of soul, *nous*, can exist in separation from the body; but he finds it difficult to say much that is clear and useful about this activity without an agent, this form without matter.

6 Logic

In this and the next two chapters we shall look at a part of Aristotle's work commonly called the *Organon*. The treatises in question are logical (in a broad sense of the word), and they were called the *Organon* – the tool or instrument – because logic was thought to be, not one of the substantial parts of philosophy, like metaphysics or natural philosophy or ethics, but rather a method or discipline useful as a tool in all enquiries, whatever their subject-matter. This is why in the traditional ordering of Aristotle's works the *Organon* comes first.

Within the *Organon* the *Categories* and *De interpretatione* come first, followed by the *Analytics*. (This is because the *Categories* deals with terms, the constituents of propositions, the *De interpretatione* deals with propositions, the constituents of syllogisms, and the *Analytics* deals with syllogisms.) The *Categories* contains a theory of categories, with an associated theory of predication, and an account of the categories of substance, quantity, relation and quality. All these matters come up again, with developments and refinements, in other works of Aristotle. The first chapters of the *De interpretatione* define the terms 'name', 'verb', 'sentence', 'statement', 'affirmation' and 'negation' (fertile seeds of later theories of grammar and meaning). The main body of the work treats of various sorts of statement and of some of their logical properties and relationships. Two chapters are an early study in modal logic, the logic of propositions involving necessity or possibility. Topics handled in the *De interpretatione* are carried further elsewhere, particularly in the *Prior Analytics*, which takes over and develops some of the ideas expounded in the *De interpretatione*, while correcting others.

The first two books of the *Analytics*, the *Prior Analytics*, study the conditions of valid deduction and in particular the syllogism. (This, Aristotle's formal logic, will be the main subject of the present chapter.) The last two books, the *Posterior Analytics*, study a special type of syllogism, the demonstrative syllogism, which is the form in which the sciences would ideally be expressed (see Chapter 7).

The remainder of the *Organon* consists of the *Topics* and the *Sophistici elenchi*. The *Topics* is an exhaustive examination of dialectical arguments.

A great range of both formal and informal types of argument are considered and – in Aristotle's characteristic manner – systematised. (Something will be said about this in Chapter 8.) The brief *Sophistici elenchi* is a work which, like the *Analytics*, remained an authoritative textbook for centuries. It is the source of most of the names still used for logical fallacies – it is a handbook of *bad* arguments.

At the end of the *Sophistici elenchi* there occurs a passage that serves as an epilogue to the other logical works also. It strikes an unusually personal note, and blends justifiable pride with agreeable modesty. Aristotle remarks that the first steps in any subject are always the most difficult, and that most contemporary branches of knowledge are building on the work of past generations.

> Of our present subject, however, it is not true to say that part had already been worked out and part had not: it did not exist at all. For the training given by the paid teachers of argument was rather like Gorgias' method. Some made their pupils learn rhetorical speeches by heart, others speeches which consisted of questions and answers, it being thought that most of the arguments pro and con were included. That is why the teaching they gave their pupils was rapid – but unskilled. It was not a skill but the products of a skill that they imparted to their pupils, although they claimed to be training them. It is as if someone claimed that he would impart knowledge of how to prevent pain in the feet, and then did not teach the cobbler's skill and the means of providing suitable footwear, but handed over shoes of various kinds: he has helped meet the person's need but he has not imparted a skill to him. Moreover, on the subject of rhetoric much had been said long before, whereas regarding reasoning we had nothing earlier to refer to, but we had to work things out over a long time by trial and error. If, therefore, when you look at it, this discipline appears to you in pretty good shape (considering the original conditions), when compared with other subjects which have grown up over the generations, then the only thing left for all of you who have followed the lectures is to pardon any omissions – and be heartily grateful for what has been discovered. (*Sophistici elenchi* 183b34)

Formal logic: Aristotle's syllogistic

Aristotle is famous for having invented or discovered the syllogism, thereby founding formal logic. Philosophers have held differing views about this achievement. Because he thought that the syllogism was not 'the great instrument of reason', John Locke poked fun at it: 'If syllogisms must be taken for the only proper instrument of reason and means of knowledge, it will follow that before Aristotle there was not one man that did or could know anything by reason; and that, since the invention of syllogisms, there is not one of ten thousand that doth. But God has not been so sparing to men to make them barely two-legged creatures, and left it to Aristotle to make them rational.' The philosopher Kant, on the other hand, looking for a secure path for philosophy, remarked in 1787: 'That logic has already, from the earliest times, proceeded upon this sure path is evidenced by the fact that since Aristotle it has not required to retrace a single step, unless, indeed, we care to count as improvements the removal of certain needless subtleties or the clearer exposition of its recognised teaching, features which concern the elegance rather than the certainty of the science. It is remarkable also that to the present day this logic has not been able to advance a single step, and is thus to all appearance a closed and completed body of doctrine.' Commentators too have been divided. While some have been impressed by the power and comprehensiveness of the Aristotelian syllogistic, others have dismissed it as being only a tiny and unimportant fragment of formal logic. Others, again, have condemned the syllogism outright as an artificial strait-jacket upon thought, a pedantic construction bearing no relation whatsoever to how the mind works.

We can return to these appraisals and comment upon them after we have seen what Aristotle's theory of the syllogism really is. This we are now in a peculiarly good position to see. The present state both of scholarship and of logic enables us to avoid major misunderstandings sometimes made in the past. Scholars have come to realise that there can be a great difference between Aristotle and his own words on the one hand, and Aristotelianism and the long tradition on the other. We must therefore study the works of Aristotle without letting our understanding be too much affected by what has been said later – by people who often had other interests, and less ability, than Aristotle, and who often had bad texts of his works and poor philological resources. On the side of logic, giant strides in mathematics and mathematical logic have been made since Kant's time. We can now locate Aristotle's logic on a larger map, and we are possessed of precise and demanding criteria by which we can estimate correctly its strength (or weakness) and its limitations. In what follows I shall not aim at a complete, or a completely rigorous, account of Aristotle's syllogistic. I want only to give an idea of what he is up to, and to indicate why his work in this area is important and remarkable.

Aristotle defines a syllogism as follows: 'A syllogism is an argument in which, certain things having been taken, something other than the things taken follows necessarily by their being so.' This is in fact a rather good account of what a valid argument is. But his official theory of the syllogism does not handle every kind of argument that would satisfy that definition. Without yet asking what the theory leaves out – and whether Aristotle realises that it does leave some valid arguments out – let us make clear what arguments it covers.

The propositions that occur in syllogisms are all of the subject–predicate (S–P) form, and they are of four types: they are either affirmative or negative and either universal or particular. Informal examples of these four types would be:

> Every man is mortal – universal affirmative   (traditionally called an
> *a* proposition)
> No man is mortal – universal negative   (*e*)
> Some man is mortal – particular affirmative   (*i*)
> Some man is not mortal – particular negative   (*o*)

I call these examples *informal* because in the rigorous working out of the theory Aristotle expresses these propositions the other way round, the predicate term before the subject term. The *a* proposition for instance is formulated 'Mortal belongs to every man', or, to generalise, 'P belongs to every S.' This technical style of formulation has certain advantages, especially in Greek, and it will be adopted in the remainder of this chapter. So the four types of proposition will be symbolised as follows: P *a* S (e.g. 'Mortal belongs to every man'), P *e* S, P *i* S, P *o* S. (When thinking of examples in ordinary English one must remember to change the order of the terms: the ordinary version of our P *a* S example is of course 'Every man is mortal', the term symbolised as P coming second.)

A syllogism contains two premises and a conclusion. If two propositions (of the kinds just mentioned) are to have any hope of yielding a conclusion, they must have a common term, called the 'middle term' (symbolised as M), and the terms of the conclusion will be the other two of the three terms contained in the premises. Since the middle term may be subject in both premises, predicate in both premises, or subject in one and predicate in the other, a syllogism will fall into one of three 'figures' as follows:

I	II	III
P M	M P	P M
M S	M S	S M
P S	P S	P S

The first premise in a figure I syllogism may of course be an *a*, *e*, *i*, or *o* proposition: P *a* M or P *e* M or P *i* M or P *o* M; and the second similarly may be M *a* S or M *e* S or M *i* S or M *o* S. Thus there are sixteen possible premise-pairs in this and in each of the three figures. But only some of these premise-pairs yield a conclusion (logically imply a third proposition). If P belongs to every M and M belongs to every S, it follows that P belongs to every S; this therefore (P *a* m, M *a* S → P *a* S) qualifies as a syllogism. (This is the syllogism traditionally labelled Barbara, because it consists of three a propositions. An example, put in ordinary English, would be: Every cat is an animal and every animal is mortal, so every cat is mortal.) However, if P belongs to every M and M belongs to some S, it does *not* follow that P belongs to every S; this therefore (P *a* M, M *i* S → P *a* S) is not a syllogism. But does this premise-pair yield some other conclusion? Yes, it does. For if P belongs to every M and M belongs to some S, it follows that P belongs to *some* S. Thus P *a* M, M *i* S → P *i* S is a syllogism. Aristotle goes systematically through all the possible premise-pairs in each figure and enquires of each pair whether or not it yields any conclusion. How does he decide the question? He takes it that a few 'moods' (i.e. premise-pairs plus conclusion) are *obviously* valid, and he gives proofs of the validity of the *other* valid moods. It is the four valid moods of the first figure that he regards as evidently valid; he shows that the valid moods in the other figures can be derived from them. To put the matter in our way, he takes the four first-figure syllogisms as *axioms* of the system, and he derives all the other syllogisms as theorems. (As a matter of fact, he later shows that all other syllogisms can be derived from just *two* of the first-figure syllogisms.)

How does Aristotle prove that these other valid moods are valid? How does he derive them from the valid moods he takes as axioms? He uses several methods, all of logical interest, but the main one is the method of 'reduction'. For my present purpose it will be sufficient to give a couple of examples. First, a direct quotation – which will serve also to illustrate the highly compressed form in which Aristotle expounds his results. Having worked through first-figure premise-pairs and picked out those which yield a conclusion, he turns to the second figure:

> When the premises are universal there will be a syllogism whenever the middle term belongs (i) to no P and every S or (ii) to every P and no S; otherwise not. [Proof of (i):] Let M be predicated of no P but of every S. Since the negative converts, P will belong to no M. But M belonged to every S. So P will belong to no S. For this has been proved already. [Proof of (ii):] Again, if M belongs to every P and to no S, P will belong to no S. For if M to no S, then S to no M; but M belonged to every P. S therefore will belong to no P. For again the first figure has been reached. (*Prior Analytics* I.5.27a3)

Let us take the two proofs in turn. In the first Aristotle wishes to show that the following is a valid mood, i.e. a genuine syllogism:

M belongs to no P	(M *e* P)
M belongs to every S	(M *a* S)
P belongs to no S	(P *e* S)

He points out that M *e* P entails P *e* M: 'the negative converts'. (You can change round – 'convert' – the order of terms in an *e* proposition without changing its truth-value.) So, clearly, M *e* P and M *a* S together entail whatever P *e* M and M *a* S together entail. But it has already been established in analysis of first-figure moods that P *e* M and M *a* S together entail P *e* S. Evidently, therefore, M *e* P and M *a* S together entail P *e* S.

This proof can be pictured as follows, the arrow standing for the relation of entailment or logical implication:

$$
\begin{array}{cc}
\text{I} & \text{II} \\
\text{P } e \text{ M} \longleftarrow \text{M } e \text{ P} \\
\underline{\text{M } a \text{ S}} & \underline{\text{M } a \text{ S}} \\
\text{P } e \text{ S} & \text{P } e \text{ S}
\end{array}
$$

The second is a more complicated example. Here Aristotle wishes to show that the following is valid:

M *a* P
M *e* S
P *e* S

It has already been established that the following first-figure mood is valid:

S *e* M
M *a* P
S *e* P

But the premise-pair M *a* P and M *e* S entails the pair S *e* M and M *a* P (since M *e* S entails S *e* M – the same move as in the previous example – and the order of premises makes no difference). So whatever S *e* M and M *a* P together entail must be entailed by M *a* P and M *e* S. So these last entail S *e* P. But that entails P *e* S (the same conversion again).

The argument can be pictured as follows:

$$
\begin{array}{cc}
\text{I} & \text{II} \\
\text{S } e \text{ M} & \text{M } a \text{ P} \\
\text{M } a \text{ P} & \text{M } e \text{ S} \\
\hline
\text{S } e \text{ P} \longrightarrow & \text{P } e \text{ S}
\end{array}
$$

The premises of the figure II argument entail those of the figure I argument, and the conclusion of the figure I argument entails that of the figure II argument. Therefore if the figure I argument is valid, so is the figure II argument.

Another way in which the reasoning here can be expressed is the following. Aristotle has to prove:

(i) If M a P and M e S, P e S (second-figure syllogism).

He already has:

(ii) If S e M and M a P, S e P (an admittedly valid first-figure syllogism).

He argues, in effect:

(iii) If M a P and M e S, M a P and S e M (by conversion of e-proposition).

(iv) If M a P and S e M, S e M and M a P (changing the order of the propositions).

(v) So if M a P and M e S, S e M and M a P (from iii and iv).

(vi) So if M a P and M e S, S e P (from ii and v).

(vii) If S e P, P e S (by conversion of e-proposition).

(i) So if M a P and M e S, P e S (from vi and vii).

'Direct reduction' proves that certain moods of other figures are valid given that we already accept as valid certain first-figure moods. The proofs – as my examples will have made clear – depend on a number of logical truths. First, there are 'rules of conversion'. In the above we made use of the rule that the negative universal converts, i.e. that A e B entails B e A. In other reductions Aristotle makes use of two other conversion-rules:

If A a B, then B i A
If A i B, then B i A

(It is *not*, of course, the case that if A o B, then B o A: some animals are not cats, but it by no means follows that some cats are not animals.) Aristotle is perfectly aware that he needs to rely on these rules, and he precedes his investigation of the syllogistic moods with a section on conversions.

> [1] If A belongs to no B, B will belong to no A [A *e* B → B *e* A]. For if to some, say C, it will not be true that A belongs to no B – for C is one of the Bs.
> [2] But if A belongs to every B, B will belong to some A [A *a* B → B *i* A]. For if to none, A will belong to no B, but it was laid down to belong to every B.
> [3] If A belongs to some B, it is necessary that B belong to some A [A *i* B → B *i* A]. For if to none, A will belong to no B.
> [4] But if A does not belong to some B, it is *not* necessary that B should not belong to some A [not: A *o* B → B *o* A]. For instance, if B is animal and A is man: man does not belong to every animal, but animal does belong to every man [i.e. not every animal is a man, but every man is an animal]. (*Prior Analytics* I.2.25a15)

It will be seen that Aristotle seeks to *prove* rules [2] and [3] by appealing to [1] ('If to none, A will belong to no B' is the rule of conversion for *e*-propositions, B *e* A → A *e* B). Thus, as in the theory of the syllogism, he aims at assuming as little as possible and deriving as much as possible. However, more is required for his derivations than [1] itself. For example, the proofs of [2] and of [3] take for granted that B *i* A and B *e* A are contradictories (so that the supposition that B *i* A is false is the supposition that B *e* A is true). Aristotle in fact assumes a number of logical truths, rules of 'immediate inference', about the interrelations of *a*, *e*, *i*, and *o* propositions: that *a* and *o* propositions are contradictory, that *e* and *i* propositions are contradictory, that A *a* B entails A *i* B, and so on. Such interrelations are studied and laid out (in the so-called Square of Opposition) in the *De Interpretatione*.

So far we have seen Aristotle deriving his syllogistic from a few syllogisms, taken as axiomatic, and a few conversion-rules, two of these being derived from the first with the aid of some assumptions about contradiction. But his proofs rely also on logical laws of a quite different kind – for example, that if *p* entails *q*, and *q* and *r* entail *s*, then *p* and *r* entail *s*. These are laws of *propositional* logic; the letters stand for complete propositions, not (like A, B, S, P, M etc. in Aristotle's syllogistic) for *terms* in propositions. In his reductions Aristotle uses such laws with facility and mastery. Consider for example the step to (v) on page 85 above, from (iii) and (iv). It relies on the following truth of propositional logic: If (*p* and *q*) entails (*p* and *r*), and (*p* and *r*) entails (*r* and *p*), then (*p* and *q*) entails (*r* and *p*). Consider also the step from (ii) and (v) to (vi) above. However, Aristotle does not explicitly state or study such logical truths, and it is because of this that his syllogistic is only a *part* of formal logic (and, as would now be thought, the lesser part). Propositional logic was discovered and developed in antiquity by the Stoics, and a battle ensued between Aristotelians and Stoics as to which 'school' had the true logic. The Aristotelians won, and propositional logic had to be rediscovered after Kant.

Before trying to evaluate Aristotle's achievement I will say just a little more about what he does in the *Prior Analytics*. Besides the direct reduction described above he uses certain other methods to establish validity – notably a kind of *reductio ad absurdum* argument: he shows that two premises entail a conclusion by appealing to the (already established) fact that the contradictory of that conclusion taken with one of those premises entails the contradictory of the other premise. He is relying here on the logical truth that if p and not-r entail not-q, then p and q entail r. For showing moods to be *in*valid Aristotle normally relies on producing counter-examples. One can indeed show an argument-form to be invalid by producing an example of an argument in that form where it is known that the premises are true and the conclusion false. But this is not really, for the logician, a satisfactory 'rejection procedure'; he would wish to *prove*, given some axioms, that such-and-such moods are invalid.

The rest of the *Prior Analytics* contains many developments on the structure so far outlined. Aristotle investigates indefatigably all kinds of interrelations among premises, premise-pairs and moods. Since he intends his logic to be of practical service, he works out which kinds of proposition one needs to look for if one is aiming at drawing a conclusion of a particular kind. He works out rules of quantity and quality (i.e. as to whether premises are to be universal or particular, affirmative or negative), rules such that all and only the moods which satisfy them are valid, i.e. are syllogisms properly speaking. For example, at least one premise must be universal, and at least one premise must be affirmative; and if the conclusion is to be negative, one premise must be negative. Aristotle shows how arguments not dressed up in syllogistic form can be re-expressed in that form, and he give rules for the correct formulation of propositions – for reducing the great variety of ordinary modes of expression to the canonical forms P a S, P e S, P i S, P o S. Further, he repeats his enquiries with respect to premises that are *modal*, i.e. premises which say, not that P belongs (or does not belong) to some (or every) S, but that it *necessarily* or *possibly* or *not possibly* belongs (or does not belong). The complications involved here are enormous, and in this (still contentious) branch of logic Aristotle does not walk quite so confidently and irreproachably as in his 'assertoric' syllogistic.

Aristotle's achievement in formal logic

First we must notice the limitations of Aristotle's achievement. The *scope* of his syllogistic is severely restricted. It handles only subject–predicate propositions, and only subject–predicate propositions of the four types *a*, *e*, *i*, and *o*. (An example of an inference falling right outside its scope is: Tom is taller than Mary and Mary is taller than Sue, so Tom is taller than Sue.) More serious even than this limitation is the fact that it is exclusively a term-logic. A complete formal logic requires both a term-logic and a propositional logic – and the latter is in fact the more fundamental of the two. It is the more general in that it deals with logical relations among propositions of any form. It is also more basic, in that it is presupposed by a term-logic. As we saw, Aristotle does (and must) rely on theses that belong to propositional logic in working out his syllogistic, notably in deriving other valid moods from those taken as axiomatic. It must therefore be allowed that his achievement in formal logic is confined to one part of term-logic, which is itself only one part – and the less fundamental part – of logic.

Within these limits, however, Aristotle's performance is admirable in ways I have tried to indicate. To put it in a word, he aims at and achieves, in the area he investigates, a high degree of system and precision, of abstraction and of rigour. The very idea of such a science of logic, an idea that now seems so obvious, was a stroke of genius. Plato, as great a philosopher and thinker as Aristotle, and with a high regard for mathematics and its systematic rigour, showed no interest in formalising the arguments and deductions made in ordinary language and in science, and was indeed inclined to regard close attention to details of terminology as a pedantic diversion from serious thought. Formal logic could not get a real start until someone conceived the aim of applying mathematical standards of exactness and rigour to the laying out of the bare bones of deductive arguments.

It is remarkable how closely Aristotle comes to achieving his aim. Three points deserve special emphasis. (i) He uses letters to stand for the terms of propositions, thus abstracting entirely in his formal exposition from the actual subject-matter of particular arguments. (ii) He adopts a consistent technical vocabulary in his systematic treatment of syllogisms. He gets away from the rich variety of ordinary language to a very limited, but precise and rigorous, form of expression. It is of course of crucial importance for the development of formal logic that absolute correctness and consistency of terminology and expression should be sought – and *not* regarded as mere pedantry. (iii) Aristotle works hard to satisfy his ideal of logic as an axiomatic system like geometry. He is ingenious in deriving most of the valid moods from those few taken as basic; and he lays bare many of the fundamental logical truths on which his derivations rely.

In the last century some influential philosophers thought that logic was the study of the laws of thought, and consequently found Aristotle's syllogistic barren and artificial: live thought does not clothe itself in such a strait-jacket. Now we recognise formal logic as allied to mathematics rather than to psychology; and the fact that Aristotle does not 'psychologise' logic, but rather 'mathematises' it, has become a ground for admiration.

Some problems

The above very simplified account has been designed to give an impression of Aristotle's formal logic as we can now understand it. Scholarly work on the text has made clear the great care Aristotle took in his terminology and formulations with a view to achieving rigour and precision and system; and developments in logic have made us fully appreciative of these qualities as cardinal virtues in a logician. It goes without saying that many problems still await the student of the *Prior Analytics*. Some are quite general philosophical problems. For example, what is the nature and status of the terms of propositions? Are they classes or concepts or universals or what? (And what *are* classes, concepts, universals?) Other difficult questions concern possibility and necessity, and the distinction – if there is one – between logical or conceptual necessity and factual or natural necessity. In the rest of this chapter I will confine myself to mentioning one or two of the less general and more technical problems that Aristotle's syllogistic raises.

First, a traditional puzzle, why does Aristotle not admit a *fourth* figure? Such a figure would be of the following pattern, different from the three set out above (page 82):

$$
\begin{array}{cc}
\text{M} & \text{P} \\
\text{S} & \text{M} \\
\hline
\text{P} & \text{S}
\end{array}
$$

There is no doubt that there are valid moods in this figure, for instance, if M *a* P and S *a* M, P *i* S. An informal example: If all tabbies (P) are cats (M), and all cats are animals (S), some animals are tabbies. Aristotle does in fact recognise such moods as valid. His successors simply added the fourth figure to the syllogistic system, without creating any difficulties. So why did he himself allow for only three figures? One traditional explanation has been psychological: it has been argued that the fourth figure moods, though no doubt from a logical point of view valid, are not ways in which we actually think or reason. From the two premises above the mind 'naturally' infers, not that some animals are tabbies, but that all tabbies are animals – and *this* argument is a *first*-figure argument. 'The answer [to the question why Aristotle does not recognise a fourth figure] is that his account of the syllogism is not derived from a formal consideration of all the possible positions of the middle term, but from a study of the way in which actual thought proceeds, and that in actual thought we never do reason in the way described in the fourth figure' (W. D. Ross).

An alternative answer to the question confines itself to logical and formal considerations. In introducing his three figures Aristotle argues, rightly, that there are only three ways in which three terms can be put together into two propositions. 'There must be a term common to both premises, and there are three possible ways. A may be predicated of C and C of B, or C may be predicated of both A and B, or both A and B may be predicated of C. Since these are our above-mentioned three figures, it is clear that every syllogism must fall under one of these figures' (*Prior Analytics* I.23.41a13). On *this* tripartite division of all possible moods, all moods with premise-pairs in which the middle term is in subject-place in one premise and predicate-place in the other fall into the same group; the traditional first and fourth figures collapse into this one group. However, when Aristotle comes to consider possible conclusions from premise-pairs and to put each syllogism into a strict 'canonical' form, he adopts the rule that the term other than the middle term which occurs in the first premise shall be the first term (i.e. the predicate-term) in the conclusion. To put the matter the other way round, if the conclusion of a syllogism has X as its first term, he writes the X-premise as the first premise. Now this rule, no doubt designed to bring regularity and order into the exposition, has the consequence of splitting up what was a single group of moods into two different figures:

I		IV	
P	M	M	P
M	S	S	M
P	S	P	S

If the *order* of premises were not laid down (by a rule connecting it with the order of terms in the conclusion) there would be no need of four figures: I and IV would become indistinguishable.

It seems, therefore, that Aristotle's omission of the fourth figure may be explained by formal considerations rather than by reference to what is natural or unnatural in reasoning. In a sense he falls between two stools.

He rightly divides up all possible premise-pairs into three groups and sets out to consider each in turn. But by adopting a rule that relates the order of the premise to the position of terms in the conclusion – in itself a sensible device – he produces the need for a *four*fold division of syllogisms, but fails to realise it. If something like this account is correct, we have to find a technical fault in Aristotle's formal logic, but we do not have to accuse him of the graver fault of mixing up psychological and logical enquires.

So much for the omission of fourth-figure moods from the systematic exposition. Another group of moods Aristotle does not list are the so-called 'weakened' moods. These are syllogisms in which a weaker conclusion is drawn than could be drawn. From the premise-pair P *a* M and M *a* S the conclusion P *a* S can be drawn; and this is a recognised first-figure syllogism. But it is also true that the conclusion P *i* S can be drawn, a weaker conclusion than P *a* S. So ought this not to be admitted as another first-figure mood: If P *a* M and M *a* S, P *i* S? Here again an explanation may be sought in either of two directions. It may be said that for practical purposes, in proofs, arguments and conversations, one never *wants* a weaker conclusion where one could draw a stronger one. Alternatively, one might suppose that it is in seeking purely logical economy that Aristotle excludes such further valid arguments as can be derived from the syllogisms he gives by a simple application of rules of immediate inference. (The above weakened mood is derivable from the strong one by the use of 'P *a* S → P *i* S'.) Most of those he gives are, as we have seen, themselves derivable from first-figure moods – but these derivations are by the methods of direct and indirect reduction, not just by a single application of a rule of immediate inference.

I turn finally to an issue that has provoked some interest recently, that of the 'existential import' of universal propositions. In modern logic the universal proposition is equivalent to the negation of an existential proposition: 'Whatever is A is B' means the same as 'It is not the case that there are some As that are not Bs.' But this last is clearly true if there are no As at all. So the universal affirmative 'Whatever is A is B' is itself true if there are no As at all. (Similarly with the universal negative: 'Nothing that is A is B' is true if there are no As at all.) The universal proposition, so construed, does not have 'existential import'. So far from its truth implying that there are some As, there *not* being any As actually guarantees its truth.

In Aristotle things are very different. As we have seen, among the rules of immediate inference which his syllogistic assumes and uses are (i) that if A *a* B, A *i* B, or, to put it informally, that if all Bs are As, some Bs are As; and (ii) that if A *e* B, A *o* B, or, to put it informally, that if no Bs are

As, some Bs are not As. Now since it is obvious that 'Some Bs are As' and 'Some Bs are not As' can be true only if there are some Bs, it follows that the universal affirmative and negative propositions which *entail* these can themselves be true only if there are some Bs. Thus the rules of immediate inference imply that universal propositions in the syllogistic do have existential import.

To ask which interpretation of the universal proposition is right may be inappropriate, in so far as each system may be internally consistent and logically impeccable. One might of course ask which comes closer to the meaning in ordinary usage of statements of the form 'All As are Bs and 'No As are Bs.' The answer is not altogether simple. 'All trespassers will be prosecuted' may surely be true even though as a matter of fact nobody will ever trespass. So it carries no existential import. However, that there will be no trespassers is surely not *sufficient* to guarantee the truth of 'All trespassers will be prosecuted.' So it is not after all equivalent to 'Nothing is both a trespasser and unprosecuted.' In more conversational contexts universal statements seem usually to carry the implication of existence. 'All my cabbages are Savoys' is a remark that can hardly be followed by 'I have no cabbages.' On the other hand, it seems odd to suggest that 'All my cabbages are Savoys' is really a compound of two different statements, 'I have some cabbages' and 'All of them are Savoys.' That I have some cabbages is something that I am taking for granted or presupposing, something that I am implying in making my remark, rather than something that I am actually asserting in making it.

The question whether Aristotle's way of handling universal propositions corresponds to ordinary conversational use is interesting, but a serious difficulty internal to his system also demands attention. Here it is, briefly put. To safeguard the immediate inference P a S $\rightarrow$ P i S we have to assume that P a S (like P i S) implies that there are some Ss. But if it does imply this, then it is not the contradictory of P o S. For both P a S and P o S will be false if there are no Ss. But we have seen that in working out reductions Aristotle uses the assumption that a and o are contradictory. So at different points in his system – in his derivations of valid moods from the axiomatic first-figure ones – Aristotle requires two inconsistent theses:

(i) P a S $\rightarrow$ P i S.

(ii) P a S contradicts P o S, i.e. if P a S is true, P o S is false, and if P a S is false P o S is true.

The most promising way out of this is provided by the distinction, already touched on, between what is asserted and what is presupposed.

When I say 'All my cabbages are Savoys' I am presupposing, not asserting, that the class 'my cabbages' has members, is not an 'empty' class. The syllogistic system *as a whole* takes for granted that *none* of the classes to be referred to in it is empty, that the kinds of thing or the properties it deals with really exist. Given that presupposition, that there are Ss and there are Ps, P *a* S does after all contradict P *o* S: either every S is a P or some S is not a P.

7 The philosophy of science

As we have seen, Aristotle is motivated in the working out of his syllogistic by a desire to systematise logic and to make clear its structure. He shows how, given the validity of a few moods, the validity of many others can be proved by the use of a few logical techniques. However, he does not explicitly discuss the project of setting out logic as a rigorous deductive structure, like Euclid's geometry. He sees himself as developing a system to serve as a tool for science, not as theorising about that system. In the *Prior Analytics* Aristotle is doing logic rather than philosophy of logic.

In the *Posterior Analytics*, on the other hand, Aristotle is not doing science but philosophy of science. The aim of the work is to analyse the concepts and the structure of the sciences, sciences which are themselves carried forward in *other* works, notably the biological ones. Book I is about demonstration and the demonstrative syllogism, that is, the kind of proof or explanation that conveys scientific knowledge or understanding. Book II deals with problems about definitions, their nature, their role in demonstration, and how they are to be established.

Demonstration and scientific knowledge

Any science will, according to Aristotle, have certain starting-points: definitions, existence-propositions and general logical truths. (Compare the starting-points of Euclid's geometry: definitions, postulates and 'common principles'.) None of these starting-points will itself be demonstrable; they will have to be grasped in some other way. The definitions will be 'real' definitions, not just verbal ones: they will give the inner or essential nature of those natural kinds that the science is about. From them will be deduced by valid syllogisms further characteristics that things of such kinds necessarily have in virtue of their essential nature. The starting-points are, as it were, the axioms of the science, and the demonstrated truths are its theorems. To have acquired a scientific knowledge or understanding of some proposition is to have demonstrated it, that is, deduced it validly from premises which are true and necessary, and which are the genuine 'causes' (i.e. are genuinely explanatory) of the conclusion in question.

We think we have scientific knowledge [*episteme*] of something whenever we think we know that the cause which explains the thing in question *is* its cause, and that it is not possible for this to be otherwise. So it is clear that having scientific knowledge is being in this sort of condition. Those who think they have scientific knowledge think that they are themselves in this condition, while those who do have it actually are. It follows that anything of which there is scientific knowledge cannot be otherwise.

Now whether there is also another type of knowledge we shall say later. [There must be if the starting-points are themselves to be knowable, and there is – *nous*: it is *nous* that grasps the indemonstrable starting-points of demonstration.] But we can at any rate say now that there is knowledge through demonstration. By a demonstration I mean a scientific syllogism, i.e. a syllogism such that one who has it has scientific knowledge of something.

If then scientific knowledge is as we were saying, it is necessary for demonstrative knowledge to depend on premises which are true and primitive and immediate, and more familiar than and prior to and causes of the conclusion . . . Without such premises there may well be a syllogism, but it will not be a demonstration, since it will not produce scientific knowledge. (*Posterior Analytics* I.2.71b9)

'Causes of the conclusion': the premises must give the real explanation of the fact mentioned in the conclusion. It is not enough that they should be true and that the conclusion should follow from them. Here is one of Aristotle's examples. Suppose that it is the nearness of the planets that explains why they do not twinkle. Now from the premises – the true premises – that the planets do not twinkle, and that non-twinkling heavenly bodies are near, we can validly deduce that the planets are near. But in doing so we do not explain or demonstrate anything; for our premises do not give the 'causes' of the conclusion. What we have is merely a 'syllogism of the *that*'. The fact that the planets are near is correctly inferred, but it is not explained by the facts from which it is inferred. The correct and explanatory order is the reverse; it is *because* the planets are near, and heavenly bodies that are near do not twinkle, that the planets do not twinkle. This is a 'syllogism of the *because*'. The fact that the planets do not twinkle is explained by the facts from which it is inferred.

Aristotle argues that the starting-points of demonstration must be *necessary*. It is possible that in such passages as the following he is guilty of some confusion. Demonstrated truths are, of course, necessarily true in that they *follow* necessarily from true premises. But is it clear that the true premises themselves, the starting-points, are *necessarily* true? What in their case would this claim amount to – since it could not mean that they followed necessarily from yet other premises?

> Since it is impossible for that of which there is scientific knowledge to be otherwise, what is known in virtue of demonstrative knowledge must be necessary. Demonstrative knowledge is the knowledge we have by having a demonstration. A demonstration therefore is a deduction [*syllogismos*] from *necessary* premises. (*Posterior Analytics* I.4.73a21)

> Demonstrative knowledge comes from necessary starting-points – for what is known cannot be otherwise. (*Posterior Analytics* I.6.74b5)

Aristotle makes various attempts to sort out the different kinds of starting-point required by a demonstrative science. Here is one such attempt.

> Some immediate deductive starting-points which cannot be proved do not *have* to be grasped by anyone who is to learn anything; these I call posits. Others, which it is necessary for anyone who is going to learn anything whatever to grasp – there are some such things – I call axioms, for this is the name we usually apply specially to them. A posit which assumes that something is, or that something is not, is a supposition; without this assumption it is a definition. For a definition is a posit – it is posited by the arithmetician that a unit is what is quantitatively indivisible – but not a supposition: what a unit is and that a unit is are not the same. (*Posterior Analytics* I.2.72a14)

One point on which Aristotle is very emphatic is that different sciences need different starting-points because of their difference of subject-matter. He rejects the idea, which he attributes to Plato, of a single comprehensive science. As in areas other than science he is insistent that one must use premises and methods appropriate to the type of question under discussion.

> One cannot give a proof by crossing over from another kind – e.g. prove something geometrical by arithmetic. For there are three things in demonstrations: (i) what is being demonstrated, the conclusion – that some attribute belongs to some kind of thing; (ii) the axioms – from which the demonstration is derived; (iii) the subject-matter, i.e. the kind of thing, whose characteristics and essential attributes are made clear by the demonstration. (*Posterior Analytics* I.7.75a38)

Aristotle's strict requirements for the premises of a demonstration seem to have an unwelcome consequence. For how can a set of necessary truths possibly provide an adequate explanation for what actually goes on in the world? How could we derive from them any understanding or knowledge of particular events and things? To put the point in another way, scientific laws alone cannot hope to give the full explanation of individual events or things, since any full explanation must include mention of facts – not laws – about the environment and about the preceding conditions in the particular case. Aristotle feels the difficulty, but the solution he offers, in the following passage, is rather obscure. The fact is that he does not wish to claim that there can be scientific knowledge or understanding of particular events or things; it is only *kinds* of event or thing about which such knowledge is possible.

> It is obvious that if the propositions from which a syllogism is derived are universal, the conclusion of such a demonstration – a demonstration in the proper sense – must itself be an eternal truth too. So there can be no demonstration of perishable things, nor scientific knowledge of them properly speaking, since the attribute does not hold of the thing universally, but at some time and in some way ... Demonstrations and knowledge of things that come about often, such as eclipses of the moon, clearly do hold always in so far as they are of a certain *type* of thing, but in so far as they do not hold always, they are [not universal but only] particular. As with eclipses, so in other cases.
> (*Posterior Analytics* I.8.75b21)

Such, in broad outline, is Aristotle's account of scientific knowledge, his philosophy of science. It might be thought that it could be of nothing but museum interest today. For (i) the science he was acquainted with and practised was vastly less powerful and sophisticated than modern science; it lacked very many of the basic ideas of today's sciences and nearly all of their quantitative techniques. Moreover, (ii) even a relatively primitive science, for example, the science known to a pre-Newtonian amateur, could surely not be properly represented as a demonstrative system of syllogisms, nor as based upon a set of definitions. The thing sounds like an absurd antique strait-jacket.

(i) That there are limits to what Aristotle could say in the area of philosophy of science is obvious. Having not the slightest idea of relativity theory or modern genetics he could not examine the special concepts involved; and he could not have understood the nature and structure of scientific theories based on and largely expressed in advanced mathematics. However, these omissions are not fatal to the philosophical claims of his work. For, as in other fields, it is often the simple and fundamental ideas or assumptions that are the most baffling or the most difficult to justify. Thus, for example, while the expert on probability-theory is advancing the frontiers with highly refined mathematical techniques, the philosopher of probability is still for most of the time worrying about the big basic puzzles of credibility, rationality, frequency and chance. In this respect philosophy of science is more like art than like science. The ideas in a play of Sophocles are in a way very simple and untechnical, but they remain profoundly interesting and illuminating, and they have not been made obsolete by advances either in empirical psychology or in dramatic techniques.

(ii) The notion that scientists occupy themselves in expounding demonstrative syllogisms based on definitions is indeed laughable. A glance at Aristotle's own scientific treatises suffices to show that his own scientific work certainly does not have such a form. The notion may have been swallowed by some of his followers, but if we turn to Aristotle himself, we find that the absurdity dissolves. For his theory of demonstration is not *offered* as an account or theory of how scientists actually proceed when at work, but rather as an outline of the *ideal* of complete knowledge at which they are aiming. No doubt the structure of proof which he suggests is too limiting. But the idea that a science aims at achieving a theory, as simple as possible, from which will be deducible as many consequences as possible, is a valuable one; and for embodying this view of the nature of a finished science Aristotle's account of demonstration deserves respect. Ironically enough, this ideal of deducibility is closer to the rigorously mathematical theories Aristotle did not know than to the more homely and less quantified theories that were available at his time.

A critic may now say: 'I allow that Aristotle was outlining an ideal for science – a guiding light; and also that the simplicity of his ideas and of his formal logic need not in themselves prevent his outline from being of interest still. But there is a more important respect in which his approach is so archaic as to make his work in this field worthless. For we all recognise that science is and is bound to remain *empirical*; that its starting-points and conclusions are not necessary truths (like the truths of logic and mathematics), but just true as a matter of fact; and that any definitions it relies upon are not 'real' definitions, but simply conventional linguistic conveniences. Aristotle, however, followed by many others after him, had the idea that human reason can 'see' (by *nous*) the necessity of certain basic truths, and can grasp the real, non-conventional truth of certain definitions. This absurd rationalism is a fatal flaw in his account of the nature and structure of science.'

There is something true in this, and something not so true. I return to definitions in a moment. The point I want to make here is that the above remarks would have sounded much more obviously correct and decisive thirty years ago than they do now. For it is no longer fashionable to draw a simple and sharp distinction between the analytic and the synthetic, between the necessary and the contingent, between conceptual truths and matters of fact. The work of Quine and other contemporaries has shown that these contrasts are altogether too crude. So while the modern philosopher will certainly be more alive than Aristotle was to the possibility of *alternative* theories or conceptual schemes, he will not for this reason wish to regard a highly general scientific theory either as a *mere* empirical hypothesis or as *just* a conventional proposal. There has been a considerable loosening-up since the heyday of logical positivism, and ideas and questions found in Aristotle are again allowable. The ideas of essence, of real definition, and of natural kinds have become once more respectable and fascinating, and some old views are in process of rehabilitation.

Aristotle's formulation of an ideal for the final structure of a science can after all be seen as a brilliant anticipation rather than as an archaism.

Definitions in science

Book II of the *Posterior Analytics* is concerned with definition; and since, as we have seen, the definitions of natural kinds are among the starting-points of sciences, we might hope that Aristotle would now tell us more about such basic definitions – how they are to be discovered and how from them important bodies of scientific truth are to be derived. In fact, however, he dwells rather upon the definition in science not of the fundamental kinds of thing, but of types of event, such as eclipse and thunder. How does the plain man's idea of an eclipse differ from the scientist's definition? Aristotle seeks to bring out the structure of scientific definitions by showing that, though not themselves demonstrable, they are related in a certain way to demonstrations. His discussion is compressed and difficult, but it raises a number of interesting points which deserve mention. Although his examples are archaic, some of his ideas will be found remarkably up to date.

Let us concentrate on the thunder example. Aristotle supposes that thunder is a noise in the clouds caused by the quenching of fire in them. This is the full, scientific definition, which incorporates the explanation (quenching of fire) of the familiar phenomenon (noise in clouds). Corresponding to it there is a demonstrative syllogism, in which the middle term is *quenching of fire*. Presumably something like this is what Aristotle has in mind:

> Noise is (caused by) quenching of fire.
> Quenching of fire is (occurs) in clouds.
> Noise is (occurs) in clouds.

The two terms in the conclusion point to the merely nominal definition of thunder – 'a noise that occurs in clouds'. But the three terms of the syllogism, suitably put together, give you the 'real' or scientific definition – 'a noise in clouds caused by the quenching of fire in them'. Since the middle term in this syllogism is the explanation of the connection between noise and clouds that is asserted in the conclusion, it is a syllogism of the 'because'. Notice that a syllogism of the 'because', which gives the reason for something, does not have the reason as its conclusion, but as its middle term. The conclusion is the fact that is explained. A syllogism of the 'that' is one which concludes to one fact from some other fact, which is however not its explanation. Compare the examples about the non-twinkling of the stars (page 95).

Scientific enquiry

Aristotle precedes his account of scientific definition by an analysis of the various questions an enquirer may ask himself and it will be convenient to base our discussion on these rather than on his exceedingly condensed final account. Here are the key passages.

> The things we seek are equal in number to those we know. And we seek four things: the '*that*', the '*why*', *whether* something is, *what* it is. (*Posterior Analytics* II.1.89b23)

> Now what we seek – and what after finding we know – are as follows. Whenever we seek the '*that*', or *whether* something is, we are seeking *whether* there is or is not a middle term for it; and whenever, having become aware either of the '*that*' or *whether* something is, we seek the reason *why*, or *what* it is, then we are seeking *what* the middle term is ... In all our searches, therefore, we seek either whether there is a middle term or what the middle term is. For the cause is the middle term, and it is the cause that we are seeking in all cases. (*Posterior Analytics* II.2.89b36)

You can know whether X is (whether a certain kind of thing exists), what X is, that p (i.e. that some proposition of the form S is P, is true), why p; and there are four corresponding questions. To ask 'What is X?' presupposes that X is; and to ask 'Why p?' presupposes that p. In all four questions what is at issue is a 'cause', an explanation, a middle term. For to ask whether S is P is to ask whether there is a term M such that S is P because it is M; to go on to ask *why* S is P is to ask what that term M is. Similarly, though this calls for further elucidation, with the question whether there is such a thing as X and the question what that thing is.

Several puzzles suggest themselves here. First, why must knowing *that* precede enquiry into *why* – and how can it, if knowing a proposition that is demonstrable involves knowing the demonstration of it? The obvious solution is to distinguish two types of knowledge or two senses in which a proposition may be 'known': the knowledge *presupposed* by enquiry into the 'because' is only 'weak' knowledge, common or garden knowledge in the undemanding everyday sense; whereas the knowledge which is achieved by discovery of the 'because' is 'strong' knowledge, scientific knowledge based on real understanding. To raise the question 'Why p?' is to take for granted that p; and, further, if an enquiry 'Why p?' is to have a chance of success, it must in fact be the case that p – otherwise there can be no answer to the question. So if an enquiry of the form 'why p?' is to be made and made with a chance of success, it is prerequisite that the enquirer should suppose that p and that he should be correct in supposing that p. These are the requirements Aristotle is insisting on. He does not claim, and of course must not claim, that strict (scientific) knowledge of p must precede discovery of the explanation of p. The enquirer starts with the true belief (or, loosely, the knowledge) that p; he ends with the knowledge of p which comes from an understanding why p must be true – he ends up knowing that p because q.

A second question: Why must knowledge that there is X (i.e. that there is such a thing as X, that there really are Xs) precede enquiry into what X is – and how can it, since surely one has to know what one is looking for in order to look for it? As with the previous question, a distinction between two types or grades of knowledge would remove the appearance of contradiction. It is, however, more illuminating to consider what may be meant by 'what X is'. We need one idea of 'what X is' that makes knowledge of it a *precondition* for the acquisition of scientific knowledge, and a different idea that makes it the actual *content* of scientific knowledge. One obvious suggestion is that the initial knowledge required is really knowledge of what the word 'X' signifies, i.e. it is purely verbal knowledge; and this suggestion is reasonable enough in the context of teaching and learning. The learner can and must be told at the start what various words mean: 'X' signifies 'Y in Z' ('thunder' means 'a noise in the clouds'). But that there actually are Xs, and what Xs really are, is shown by the demonstration the learner is subsequently given; he is not required to assume at the start that there are Xs. However, if we turn from the teaching and learning of existing scientific knowledge and consider instead the discovery and the development of a science, the position is very different. Here suppositions of actual existence do have to be made with regard to items later to be proved to exist. An investigator must believe – and truly – that Y is in Z (e.g. noise occurs in clouds) if he is to bring to a successful conclusion the enquiry 'why is Y in

Z?' When he has done this he will understand that Y is in Z because of M (the middle term, the explanation). If we transform these propositions into definitions, we have 'Y in Z' as the investigator's initial definition of what X is (X, an actual phenomenon, not 'X', the word), and 'Y in Z because of M' as his final definition which incorporates the real explanation of the phenomenon in question

According to this account the investigator who is to reach a real definition, full knowledge of what X is, must start off with a grasp of part of that definition – 'having something of the actual thing' in Aristotle's words – 'e.g. of thunder, that it is a sort of noise in the clouds; of eclipse that it is a sort of privation of light; of man, that he is a sort of animal . . .'. Here one may reasonably feel doubts. An investigator who is to end up with an understanding of some kind of thing or type of event must certainly start with an idea sufficient to guide him; only if he has some way of picking out Xs (with at least some success) will he be able, by studying them, to discover their true nature. But it is surely not necessary that his original guiding idea should survive intact as part of the real definition finally achieved. Distinguish between the following: (i) the starting-point must be a grasp of part of the real definition of X (knowledge, in fact, of the conclusion that will be demonstrated eventually in the demonstrative syllogism corresponding to the complete definition); (ii) the starting-point must be a grasp of X via some feature or features of X which distinguish Xs sufficiently to enable the investigator to study more or less the right items, and so to advance to an understanding of what X really is. To take an example from more recent discussions: we now know what measles is, i.e. (to put it crudely) what causes a certain particular condition of the body. Long before this was known the word 'measles' was used, and it was applied on individual occasions because of an easily recognised group of symptoms. It may now be clear that some of the cases earlier lumped together as measles were in fact a different disease and not cases of measles at all; measles perhaps is not the only disease that shows such symptoms, they are also occasionally found in association with a quite other bodily disease and cause. Aristotle is right to see much scientific enquiry as movement from a rough idea to a full understanding of what some kind of thing or type of event is; but to be more realistic he should allow that the original 'rough idea' may be very rough, not necessarily a grasp of part of the real definition, since the final scientific definition (of thunder, of measles, of the cucumber, of the electron) may not contain the terms by which X was originally identified and defined.

A third question: Granted that the scientific investigator has to know (in some sense) that *p* (or that there are Xs) if he is to ask the question

'Why *p*?' (or 'What is X?'), *how* does he come to know this, and *how* subsequently is the advance to the knowledge why *p* (or what X is) achieved?

It might be supposed that the fact from which the scientific investigator starts (*p* or that there are Xs) is a plain fact, and that knowledge of it is provided by sense-perception, or rather by sense-perception and experience – for it will not be a singular proposition but a general one, not an individual item but a type or class of items, about which the investigator's question ('Why *p*?', 'What is X?') is asked. However, the mere knowledge or supposition that *p* (where *p* is a generalisation) or that there are Xs is not enough. The investigator must suppose also that *p* is a *scientifically explicable* truth, derivable from basic scientific laws or starting-points, if he is to think appropriate the question 'What laws explain *p*?' And he must suppose that Xs constitute a scientifically explicable class of events of phenomena, a sort of 'natural kind', if he is to think appropriate the question 'What is the causal explanation of there being Xs?' No 'because' can be found for accidental truths or for casual concomitances; and it is only if one supposes that there *is* a 'because' that one will ask what it is. Thus the necessary presupposition of the scientist's enquiry 'Why *p*?' is not just that *p* is true, but that the truth of *p* can be given a scientific explanation – not just that *p*, but that explicably-*p*. And if I ask the question 'What *is* thunder?' in a scientific sense (using what has recently been called 'the "is" of theoretical identification'), I am assuming not only that noises occur in clouds – that thunder as ordinarily tested for and spoken of occurs – but further that there really is such a single scientific thing as thunder, that observed cases are cases of one real kind of event with one scientific explanation.

We can now see why Aristotle asserts that the question whether *p* is true or whether X exists is the question whether there is a cause or a middle term. The question whether S is P is the question whether there is some term M such that S is P because it is M; and the question whether there is such a thing as Y in Z is the question whether there is a term M such that Y is in Z because of M. On the face of it these identifications are absurd. But when we remember that what is afoot is analysis of scientific enquiry we can readily understand why Aristotle makes them. For within scientific discourse it is only non-accidental propositions or concomitances that are of interest. To ask a (scientific) 'Why *p*?' is to assume the (scientific) truth of *p*, and to ask the (scientific) 'What are Xs?' is to assume the existence of Xs as (scientific) entities. Aristotle's highly compressed account perhaps conflates two ideas that should be distinguished – coming to believe that *p*, and coming to believe that *p* is scientifically explicable (or: coming to believe that there are Xs, and coming to believe that Xs constitute a scientific 'kind'). His point, however, is valid: the precondition for the investigator's enquiry 'Why *p* ?' is indeed the supposition that there is a middle term for *p*; and to ask what Xs really are is to assume that there is a scientific explanation for the combination of features we see in Xs (e.g. for noise in clouds).

But how can anyone be *justified* in making the move from *p* to explicably-*p before* finding out the explanation? Aristotle speaks blithely of becoming aware, or recognising, or grasping, that there is a middle term, and of then going on to enquire what it is. He does not tell us how we become aware, what leads us to suppose that there is a middle term, why and with what justice we go from *p* to explicably-*p* or from the belief that *p* is true to the belief that it is necessarily true. Perhaps however this is not a damaging criticism. For he is analysing the structure of science, not giving practical advice. That an investigator must assume there to be an explanation in terms of scientific laws if he is to ask the scientific 'Why?', and that his assumption must be correct if the question is to permit of an answer, are statements about the logical relations of certain questions and answers; they do not purport to illuminate the general conditions for coming to correct assumptions, let alone to guide us to the acquisition of correct assumptions in individual cases.

What does in fact give confidence that some proposition or concomitance is scientifically explicable? The most important general point is surely this, that at any given stage in scientific progress the laws and connections already reliably established provide the framework, and they are used as guides to determine the likelihood that some newly observed conjunction of features or events is law-governed. Aristotle does not, as far as I know, expressly state this principle, but his practice, naturally enough, illustrates it. Where a familiar kind of explanation can be envisaged for some fact or phenomenon, it is reasonable to expect there to be one; it is an objection to a suggested explanation if it can be described as eccentric or outlandish.

Once he has come to think that *p* is explicable, or X definable, how does the investigator proceed in order to discover the explanation or definition? Here again Aristotle's own practice, in various fields of science and philosophy, will provide the main evidence for his views. But a few general points about possible outcomes of the investigation are made or suggested in the *Posterior Analytics*, and these are possibilities which the investigator will have to bear in mind from the start. I will mention four such possibilities.

It may be found that the original question requires to be broken down into two or more questions; there is, it emerges, no *single* explanation of the original proposition *p*. There are two main types of case. (i) We asked why Ss are Ps. But it may emerge that there are two kinds of S, and that the reason why S_1s are Ps is different from the reason why S_2s are Ps. (ii) We asked why Ss are Ps. But if Ss are As that are Bs, and Ps are Cs that are Ds, the explanation why Ss are Ps may break down into two explanations; As are Cs because they are Ms, and Bs are Ds because they are Ns (Why do my hybrid roses suffer from early blackspot? Roses suffer from blackspot because . . .; hybrids develop early because . . .).

The original question may need revision for other reasons, for example: (iii) We asked why S_1s are Ps. But it may be that the only explanation of their being Ps is the explanation why in general all Ss (not just S_1s) are Ps. So there is no matching or 'commensurate' cause for the connection between being an S_1 and being a P (Why do hybrid roses get blackspot? There is no special reason why *hybrid* roses get blackspot. Roses get blackspot because . . .). Aristotle has a good deal to say about cases of this kind: explanation should always be commensurate, science is concerned with what belongs to a thing 'in itself', because it is precisely what it is. He has very much less to say about another range of cases where the investigator's original question proves to require revision and reformulation. (iv) We asked why Ss are Ps. But it is really Ts that are Ps (and we can discover why they are). Ss or most Ss may happen to be Ts, and if so Ss or most Ss are in fact Ps; but this is not a truth derivable from the laws or starting-points of the science. 'Ss are Ps' cannot get a properly scientific explanation, but in the course of trying to explain it we shall come to see instead that, and why, Ts are Ps. (Compare what was said about measles above: the set of cases we look at when we originally ask 'What *is* this disease? What causes it?' may contain some which we later decide not to be the same disease at all. So in a way we replace our original question, that could not be answered, since not all the cases we spoke of did have a common cause, by another question, about a revised set of cases, a question that can be answered.)

Aristotle's ideal of explanation

Can we get a clear idea of the *ideal* of definition and explanation to which Aristotle's theory points? As is his wont, he uses a very few highly simplified examples to bring out certain points, leaving us to make such additions and qualifications as are necessary to accommodate other essential features of his theory. Thus the premises of our thunder-syllogism do not look much like the basic definitions or existence-propositions which are supposed to be the starting points for demonstrative syllogisms. We can, however, see how the explanation of thunder would be carried forward in accordance with Aristotle's general principles. Thunder is a noise caused by quenching of fire in clouds. But what *is* noise? What *is* quenching of fire? What *are* clouds? Noise (he says) is 'a certain movement of the air'. The account of quenching and of clouds will doubtless involve the four basic powers that characterise the four basic elements, together with highly general laws of action and reaction. So a final explanation why thunder occurs and what it really is will show it to be a case of very simple laws or connections that are widely exemplified and easily understood. If the quenching of fire is (say) the departure of a certain kind of hot and dry from a surrounding wet and cold mass, and the clouds in which thunder occurs are such a wet and cold mass surrounding that kind of hot and dry, the occurrence of thunder may be seen to be necessary. But it is doubtful whether this could be a final explanation. It seems unlikely that among the indemonstrable starting-points of a science there should be the assumptions that such departures occur and that such masses exist. Simple laws might be expected to explain why, given that there are the four basic powers, such masses must form and such departures must occur. So the quest will go on for the fewest and simplest starting-points capable of explaining all the truths of the science in question.

It would be wrong to suggest that science is, according to Aristotle, just a matter of explanation in terms of physics and chemistry. As we have already seen, the scientist is concerned with final causes and the good, not only with efficient causes and the necessary. The biologist, in particular, will need starting-points of a very different kind from those adequate for the meteorologist investigating thunder. The *Posterior Analytics* does not tell us what those starting-points may be; nor is it easy to apply what is said about the definition of such phenomena as thunder and eclipse to the definition of animal and plant species. Nevertheless, we can safely credit Aristotle with the important idea that sciences aim at generalisation and simplicity, and with a recognition of the role and importance of definitions in scientific enquires and theories.

8 Philosophical method

A good deal has been said in other chapters about Aristotle's way of doing philosophy, and illustrations have been given. In this chapter I should like to take up one particular question: how, according to Aristotle, can 'starting-points' (*archai*) be discovered?

William James described human experience as 'a buzzing, blooming, confusion'. We live in a world that is familiar but in many ways bewildering, full of variety and change and complexity. Both the scientist and the philosopher look for underlying simplicities of one sort or another, to serve as starting points for explanations and to give us understanding of the world and of ourselves. Here is how Aristotle puts it at the beginning of his series of lectures on natural philosophy:

> In all fields of enquiry scientific knowledge [real understanding] of things that have principles, causes or elements, results from discovering these. We think we have knowledge of a thing when we have discovered its first causes and first principles, and have taken it back to its elements. So in seeking knowledge of nature we must obviously start by trying to get clear about principles.
>
> The natural route is from what is clearer and more easily known to us [daily experience], to what is more knowable and clearer in its own nature [basic principles and ideas] – for the two are not the same. This, therefore, is the procedure we must adopt, advancing from what is less clear by its nature but clearer to us, to what is by nature clearer and more knowable. The things that are to start with clear and plain to us are complex, composite things; it is only later and as a result of analysing them that we come to know their elements and principles. (*Physics* I.1.184a10)

There are, of course, various different *kinds* of starting-point that may be sought and would give understanding. As we saw in Chapter 7, Aristotle claims that any ideal and complete science would derive from *archai* of three kinds: definitions, logical truths, and existence-propositions. These would be the starting-points for all the demonstrations in that science; they would be its basic *premises*. In his own work, however, when he is trying to get to the fundamentals of some field of enquiry, he is usually engaged in picking out and elucidating the basic *ideas* of the subject, trying to provide a satisfactory and illuminating conceptual framework rather than premises from which deductions are to be made. So, for example, his work in *Physics* I and II on form and matter, on necessity and chance, and on the four causes, does not produce premises for syllogisms. Rather, Aristotle is isolating, clarifying and refining key ideas which are obscurely present in, or implied by, ordinary ways of talking. Similarly with more limited enquires, for instance his treatment of time in *Physics* IV: he does not end up with premises for a science of time, but with an account of time (and of related concepts) that gives understanding and insight.

This, then, is one broad distinction: starting-points may be basic propositions or they may be key concepts. Another distinction we should no doubt make is that between *archai* of sciences, to be sought by scientific investigations, and *archai* of philosophy, to be sought by philosophical methods. Without going any further we can see that the question 'How are starting-points to be discovered?' is too vague for comfort – the answer may well depend on the *sort* of starting-points being looked for and on the *sort* of subject-matter involved. In what follows I shall first report what Aristotle says in *Posterior Analytics* II.19 as to how the starting-points of demonstrative sciences are grasped. I shall then discuss his remarks in the *Topics* about the role of dialectic in establishing philosophical *archai*.

The starting-points of science

We have seen how Aristotle's account of demonstrative science, in the *Posterior Analytics*, makes it all derive from indemonstrable starting-points. The work is not concerned with the procedure for making scientific discoveries, but with the form a finished science would take. It shows how, given the starting-points, everything else will be deducible. But how are the starting-points themselves to be obtained? In the last chapter of the work Aristotle offers an account of a development leading to the grasp of *archai*, and gives a name, *nous*, to the power of grasping them.

Aristotle begins by asking whether the relevant pieces of knowledge, the indemonstrable *archai*, are innate and present in us all along, or whether they are acquired by us in some way.

To suggest that we have them all along is absurd – that we actually possess such pieces of knowledge, knowledge superior to demonstration, without noticing it. If, however, we acquire them, not having had them earlier, how could we come to know them and learn them if we had no pre-existing knowledge? That is impossible, as we said in speaking of demonstration ['All teaching and all learning come about from pre-existing knowledge' – the first sentence of the *Posterior Analytics*]. It is evidently impossible, therefore, *either* for us to have them all along *or* for us to acquire them if we are ignorant and lack every sort of knowledge. It follows that we must already have *some capacity* (of a lower quality and value than the knowledge to be acquired). (*Posterior Analytics* II.19.99b26)

Aristotle now explains how knowledge develops from sense-perception. It is not that men have innate *ideas*, but that they have innate *capacities*: they can perceive, remember, notice similarities, form general ideas, and grasp universals.

This capacity does in fact belong to all animals, since they have an inborn power of discernment, which is what is called perception. In some animals retention of the percept occurs, in others it does not. For those in which it does not occur . . . there is no knowledge outside the perceiving; but others can, after perceiving something, still hold it in their minds. And after many such occasions a further difference comes about: some come to have a *logos* [an 'account' or general idea] from retaining such things, while others do not.

From perception, then, there comes memory, and from memory – when memory of the same thing occurs often – experience; for many such memories make a single experience. And from experience, or from the whole universal that has come to rest in the mind – the one distinct from the many, whatever is one and the same in all the various things – there comes a principle of skill or a scientific knowledge, of skill if it concerns becoming, of scientific knowledge if it concerns what is.

Thus the states in question [i.e. of knowing the starting-points] neither belong in us already in a determinate form, nor come about from other states that are more highly cognitive than they; but they come about from perception. It is as in a battle when a rout occurs: if one man makes a stand another does and then another, until they reach their starting-point [the point from which they can start to counter-attack? or the point from which they were first driven back?]. The mind is of such a nature as to be capable of this.

What we have just said but not said clearly, let us say again. When one of the undifferentiated things [*infimae species*, like man or horse] makes a stand, a first universal is in the mind; for what one perceives is the particular thing, but perception is *of* the universal – e.g. of a man, not of Callias the man. [Perception tells you that you are looking at a tall, dark man with blue eyes. But that this man *is Callias* is not something immediately given by sense-perception.] Again a stand is made in these, until the uncompounded universals stand – such and such an animal, then animal, and so on. Clearly, therefore, it is by induction that we have to get to know the first things. For that is how perception too implants the universal in us. (*Posterior Analytics* II.19.99b34)

Aristotle now looks for the right label to attach to the distinctively human power of grasping universals, including those required as starting-points for sciences.

Of the intellectual dispositions by which we grasp truth, some are always true, while others (such as opinion and reasoning) can be false. Scientific knowledge and *nous* are always true, and no kind of state except *nous* is more accurate than scientific knowledge, and the starting-points of demonstrations are more knowable than their conclusions. There cannot, therefore, be scientific knowledge of the starting-points, and since nothing can be more true than scientific knowledge except *nous*, *nous* must be of the starting-points. (*Posterior Analytics* II.19.100b5)

Aristotle's chapter is interesting and has been influential, but it does not go far towards explaining how the starting-points of sciences are to be grasped. What it does explain is the gradual formation in the mind of general or abstract ideas, the grasp of concepts and of meanings. But the question remains, how can we get from ordinary concepts (derived from sense-experience in the way he described) to the precise and clearly defined terms required for scientific knowledge? *How* are we to discover – and be sure that we have discovered – the real definitions of natural kinds, or the scientific definitions of such events as eclipses and thunder? Aristotle does not tell us a method that we can adopt in conscious research directed to establishing such basic truths. Instead he provides us with a psychological essay; he describes how various mental processes and faculties lead to the forming of general ideas.

Dialectic and philosophy

In the *Topics* Aristotle systematises 'dialectic', the practice of arguing according to certain rules, for or against any given proposition. This dialectic is very much like the sort of discussion found in Plato's Socratic dialogues – the 'Socratic *elenchus*' – in which Socrates probes and tests a proposition put forward by someone else, often showing it to be inconsistent with other beliefs which the speakers accept. Aristotle distinguishes four main types of question, and correspondingly of proposition: Is A the definition of B, or the genus of B, or a necessary property of B, or an accident (a contingent, non-necessary feature) of B? Different kinds of argument and counter-argument are appropriate for the various types of question, and he works them out with many examples and in sometimes boring detail. More interesting to us than the detail is the whole idea of argument that relies on probability, analogy and other such devices, common in ordinary discussion and persuasion, though not parts of a strict formal logic. The *Topics* comes close in places to the 'informal logic' of which Gilbert Ryle spoke (in *Dilemmas*, chapter VIII), and close therefore to giving a sort of theory of live philosophical discussion – which the *Analytics* does not give. The second general feature of dialectic, which will deserve closer attention in a moment, is the requirement in it that arguments should be based upon and appeal to *endoxa* – opinions that are held or have been held, either by most people or by notable people worth attending to. A disputant in the game of dialectic will be a failure if, to keep his end up, he has to rely on the assertion of what goes against common sense and has no backing from any reputable authority.

What is the *use* of dialectical skill? If we are familiar with recognised views on many matters and are practised in arguing the pros and cons of any view, we are better equipped to win arguments. In all serious enquiries, moreover, an ability to see both sides, and to be puzzled as to how different views can be reconciled, is an important condition for progress. Aristotle makes a third large claim for dialectic:

> It is also useful for getting to the first things in each science. For it is not possible to say anything about them on the basis of the science's own starting-points, since the starting-points themselves come first and are the basis for everything else. It is through the accepted opinions [*endoxa*] on each matter that *they* [the starting-points] must be dealt with. And this procedure belongs solely or especially to dialectic. For dialectic, by examining and testing, affords a way of reaching the starting-points of all branches of enquiry. (*Topics* I.2.101a36)

The procedure of working from *endoxa*, through discussion of conflicting views and of problems (*aporiai*), towards something clear and certain, is a procedure that Aristotle often recommends and regularly adopts. One clear statement of it was given in Chapter 2 (page 12). Here are a few more.

For those who wish to be safe from difficulties it is useful to go through all the difficulties very carefully. The subsequent freedom from difficulty results from resolving the previous difficulties; and one cannot untie a knot if one does not know of it. Difficulty in our thinking points to a 'knot' in the subject-matter; in so far as our thought is in difficulties, its condition is like that of a bound man; in neither case is it possible to go forward. This is why one should have surveyed all the problems beforehand. People who embark on an enquiry without first going through the difficulties are like travellers who do not know where they have to go. Such a person does not even know whether he has at any given time found what he is looking for or not, because to him the end is not clear, whereas to someone who has first gone through the difficulties it is clear. Further, one is bound to be in a better position to judge if one has heard all the arguments on both sides of the case. (*Metaphysics* B.1.995a27)

We must try to conduct the enquiry in such a way that it will be made clear what place is, and that as a result the puzzles about it will be solved, and the attributes commonly thought to belong to it will be shown to belong to it – and further, that the reason for the difficult puzzles about it will be evident. For that is the most satisfactory kind of treatment of any topic. (*Physics* IV.4.211a7)

Let us first go through the views others held; for the proofs of one theory are difficulties for the contrary theory. Besides, those who have first heard the arguments on the other side will be more likely to have confidence in what we are going to say. We shall be less open to the charge of trying to win our case by default. Indeed those who are to judge the truth satisfactorily should be arbitrators rather than parties to the dispute. (*De Caelo* I.10.279b5)

Aristotle holds that what is generally believed is likely to have some truth in it, and that the views of the wise are also not likely to be entirely wrong. 'Everyone has something to contribute.' So a close survey of 'opinions' will both throw up problems and provide much material for solving them. The solution will preserve whatever was true in the various conflicting views, while filtering away what was unclear, exaggerated or erroneous. (If possible, we should explain how and why erroneous ideas came to be held.) Sometimes a distinction will be drawn, or an ambiguity brought to light, with the consequence that we can accept both of two apparently opposed views, provided that they are suitably interpreted.

It may be thought that this sort of procedure is more appropriate to some branches of knowledge than to others. It may even be suggested that it is not appropriate to any branch of *knowledge*, but that it is only an easy armchair way of bringing spurious clarity into a lot of opinions many of which are very possibly quite false. However, we can recognise a close relation between Aristotle's dialectic and our 'analytical philosophy' – philosophy concerned to clarify and lay bare the system of concepts which we use and which our language expresses. It is not the object of such a philosophy to shake up our way of seeing things, or to get access to a reality lying behind the veil of mere appearance; it is descriptive, not revisionary. Much of Aristotle's work is of this type – whether he is attacking quite small and definite problems or investigating the under-lying structure of whole realms of talk and thought (e.g. thought and talk about change, time, etc. in the *Physics*). In investigating some (familiar) topics he starts from an examination of what ordinary people commonly say. In others it is the rival theories of previous philosophers that provide the starting-point for puzzle and argument.

The great difference between Aristotle's conceptual investigations and those of recent philosophy is that he does not entertain the possibility of there being *alternative* conceptual schemes of equal validity and applica-bility. He supposes that the structure of Greek language and thought *is* the structure of reality. Close acquaintance with languages and cultures very different from our own, and increased concern about the subjectiv-ity of experience, have both contributed to the more relativistic and more modest view we now take about the conclusions of our investigations. Aristotle was modest enough to think that the truth was to be discovered by reflection on what others said and thought, and not by the exercise of some private and privileged insight. But he was able to suppose – and this sounds rather arrogant to us – that clarification and analysis might be brought to a satisfactory completion, and final knowledge thereby reached. (It was some of his successors, rather than he himself, who spoke as though he had actually attained this goal, and settled every question.)

In philosophy, then, there is some merit in Aristotle's claim that dialectic is the way to reach the 'first things' or 'starting-points', that is, to discover and elucidate the key ideas and the structure of our thought about the world. But what about the particular natural sciences? Surely here the procedure of dialectic has no serious place? Arguing to and fro, and developing puzzles, may play a part in research, but the collecting of evidence, and making of experiments, is surely what is essential – and if previous views (of laymen or of specialists) are upset, no matter. There seems to be a great contrast between sifting and clarifying what people think – sitting around arguing – and discovering scientific truths by induction from carefully observed facts. Does Aristotle really credit dialectic with both tasks? The following points are worth bearing in mind.

(i) *Endoxa* include not only widely held beliefs of ordinary folk but also the views of any notable group or distinguished individual. In a relatively 'scientific' area, where there are experts who have looked into the facts carefully, the views of experts will naturally be of primary interest, and the opinions of the layman will carry little weight (though we should of course like to understand why those opinions have been adopted). In this way the observed facts on which the experts base their views are – indirectly – fed into the dialectical process.

(ii) Aristotle uses one and the same formula to cover both the explanation of observed facts by scientific laws or theories and the eliciting of clear and consistent concepts from conflicting or confused opinions: he speaks of starting from and 'saving' the *phenomena*. He can use this formula because the term '*phenomena*' (like '*endoxa*') has a wide range of application. It means 'appearances' – both in the sense of what may be observed, how things look, etc., and in the sense of what seems to be true, opinions that are held. When Plato in his famous injunction to the astronomers told them to produce the simplest theory that would 'save the *phenomena*', he referred to the visible astronomical facts, which a good theory had to start from, be consistent with, and explain. But in other enquiries it can be widely held beliefs and things commonly said that *are* the facts, what we have to start from; and we aim at a 'theory' that will enable us to understand why these things are said and believed, and to grasp the system of interrelated concepts that are expressed in, or implied by, these ordinary beliefs and statements.

The object of *all* serious investigation is to move from particular facts that are near to us but not clearly understood to general truths or ideas that are difficult to work out but clear when grasped, and that give us understanding of those original facts. Investigations will be of different types, because there are different types of fact. But in every case the process is designed to 'save the *phenomena*' – the original facts, whether they are facts about ordinary language, about common beliefs or about the physical world – by developing a simple explanatory theory that covers them all and makes each intelligible.

(iii) This last point may seem a purely verbal way of closing the gap, by blurring the contrast between a scientific enquiry proper and a merely conceptual one – between science and analytical philosophy. But perhaps in any case this contrast is not really quite so sharp and absolute. Scientific ideas and discoveries have their effects upon ordinary concepts, while these themselves exercise a powerful influence on scientific investigations. We spoke earlier, in discussing Aristotle's work on definition, of the movement from a workaday understanding of a term like 'thunder' or 'measles' to the scientific understanding encapsulated in a 'real' definition. Such a movement involves a certain interplay between ordinary language, experience and concepts, and scientific language, observation and theory. Taking this into account we may be more inclined to praise Aristotle for not making a sharp contrast between science and philosophy than to blame him for bringing them too closely together.

(iv) Finally, a reminder of a point made before (page 11). However strong his trust in reasoning, Aristotle frequently insists on the need to gather adequate evidence *before* starting to argue and theorise. He collected – or got others to collect – a mass of facts about the constitutions of Greek city-states as a basis for his political theory. He drew together a vast amount of material about animals – derived from observations and dissections – before writing the biological treatises which give the explanations and theories about animal structure, behaviour and generation. (Many of his detailed observations have excited the admiration and wonder of biologists.) He is anxious not to be over-hasty in adopting a theory, and he recognises that one must adjust one's confidence to the quality of the evidence – and be prepared to be shown wrong by further evidence:

> This then is the way in which bees appear to be generated, judging from theory and from the supposed facts about bees. However the facts have not yet been sufficiently grasped; and, if ever they are, the evidence of the senses must then be believed rather than theories – and theories only if their deliverances agree with the observed facts. (*De generatione animalium* III.10.760b27)

It is only the investigator who has steeped himself in the evidence who will hit on hypotheses and theories that apply to the whole range of facts and explain them:

> Without experience one cannot take a comprehensive view of the admitted facts. That is why those who have lived with the subject – are 'at home' with nature – are better able to propose principles or starting-points capable of covering a wide field, whereas those who have done a lot of theorising without looking at the facts are only too ready to propound views on the basis of just a few observations. (*De generatione et corruptione* I.2.316a5)

9 Metaphysics

Aristotle's *Metaphysics*, from which a whole branch of philosophy takes its name, consists of a number of treatises or lecture-courses, not all written at the same time, which were brought together by a later editor. He gave to this collection the title 'Metaphysics' because the topics discussed come, in a systematic ordering, after (*meta*) the philosophy of nature (*physics*). They are mainly topics of a highly general character about reality as a whole, and about the ultimate analysis and explanation of what there is. A summary of the *Metaphysics* will give an idea of its scope.

Book A – the books of the *Metaphysics* are commonly designated by letters of the (Greek) alphabet – argues that philosophy seeks 'causes', i.e. it seeks to understand. A survey of predecessors confirms that there are no more than four kinds of cause or explanation, those mentioned in the *Physics* (page 36 above). Book B sets out fifteen problems or *aporiai*, giving arguments on both sides. (For example, are there any substances other than those we can perceive? Are the 'first principles' of substances the various kinds to which they belong, their species and genera, or rather the constituents of which they are composed?) In Book Γ Aristotle gives an account of metaphysics (or, as he himself calls it, 'first philosophy'), explaining that it investigates being as such; and then proceeds to discuss the primary axioms that apply to whatever there is and are taken for granted by all particular sciences. He concentrates on the law of contradiction – that the same thing cannot be both true and not true at the same time. No proof of this can be expected, since any rational argument has to assume it; but Aristotle tries to make clear to anyone who claims to say anything meaningful that he cannot help assuming the law. He also here refutes the notorious doctrine of Protagoras that how things appear is how they are – so that the same thing may be both hot (because it appears hot to me) and not hot (because it appears not hot to you). Book Δ is a philosophical lexicon, in which various senses or applications of some key terms ('cause', 'being', 'accidental', 'one', 'quality' etc.) are laid out. Book E offers a further account of the subject-matter of 'first philosophy', and deals briefly with accidental being and with being as truth. Books Z and H contain difficult and probing discussions of substance and essence; of matter and form; of definition; of individuation; and of existence. Book Θ examines the concepts of possibility, potentiality, and power on the one hand, and of actuality and activity on the other. Book I discusses unity, plurality and related notions. (K just contains recapitulations of passages from some other books of the *Metaphysics*, together with some extracts from the *Physics*.) Λ contains an outline account of the world of perceptible, changing substances, and then turns to the question whether there is also an eternal, non-perceptible, unchanging substance. These chapters contain the main evidence for Aristotle's mature theology. Books M and N examine critically the views of Plato and others on the existence of immaterial substances, whether Platonic Forms or mathematical objects, and also their theories as to the 'principles' of such substances.

It will be seen that the *Metaphysics* deals with a very wide range of questions. Many of its themes and ideas are to be found also in other parts of Aristotle's philosophy, and I refer to them in other chapters. In this chapter I shall first say a few words about Aristotle's concept of 'first philosophy', then discuss briefly some of his main thoughts on being and substance, and finally outline his theological position.

First philosophy

In *Metaphysics* Γ.1 Aristotle distinguishes first philosophy from all the special sciences on the ground that it studies the whole of what there is, 'being *qua* being'.

> There is a branch of knowledge that studies being qua being, and the attributes that belong to it in virtue of its own nature. Now this is not the same as any of the so-called special sciences, since none of these enquires universally about being qua being. They cut off some part of it and study the attributes of this part – that is what the mathematical sciences do, for instance. But since we are seeking the first principles, the highest causes, it is of being *qua* being that we must grasp the first causes. (*Metaphysics* Γ.1.1003a21)

In Γ.2 Aristotle points out that 'being' like 'healthy' has a variety of uses, but all related to one central point. If we say of a man, of a diet, of a complexion that they are healthy, what this means is not the same in every case: the man is healthy in that he enjoys health, the diet in that it produces health, the complexion in that it displays health. Yet clearly these uses of 'healthy' form a closely-knit family, and there can be and is a single science of health. Similarly, all sorts of things can be said to be, but what this 'being' amounts to varies: for things other than substances being is being the quality of a substance, or being in some other way a feature of or related to a substance. Substances are the primary, independent existents. So there can after all be a single science of being, and it will be primarily concerned with substances.

> There are many ways in which things may be said to 'be', but always with reference to one definite kind, and not by mere ambiguity. Other words are used in the same sort of way. For example, everything that is 'healthy' has reference to health, either from its preserving health or producing it, or being a symptom of health, or because it possesses it. Again, whatever is 'medical' has reference to medical science, one thing because it has the science, another because it is suited to it, another because it is a product of the science. So, too, there are many ways in which things are said to 'be', but all refer to one starting-point: some things are said to be because they are substances, others because they are affections of a substance, others because they are a process towards a substance, or destructions or privations or qualities of a substance ... As, then, there is a single science that deals with everything that is healthy, so in the other cases also. For it is not only things that have a single common character which are investigated by a single science, but also things that are related to a common character; indeed these too do in a way have a single common character. It is clear then that it is the work of one science to study the things that are qua things that are. But everywhere science deals chiefly with what is primary, i.e. that which other things depend on and which explains how they are spoken of. So if this is substance, it will be the principles and causes of *substances* that the philosopher must grasp. (*Metaphysics* Γ.2.1003a33)

In Γ, then, Aristotle has first defined first philosophy as a highly general study of being qua being (and of its attributes): and he has then narrowed it down by saying that since substance is the primary form of being, first philosophy will be primarily concerned with *substantial* being and with its causes and principles. In E.1, having mentioned physics and mathematics as two theoretical sciences, Aristotle introduces a further and more fundamental theoretical science, theology, which is concerned with what is a substance and exists separately (unlike mathematical objects) and is changeless (unlike physical objects). *This* idea of 'first philosophy' seems very different from that outlined in Γ. How can one reconcile the view that first philosophy is universal, and studies all being, with the view that it is first because it studies a particular substance (god)? At the end of the following passage Aristotle tries to bridge the gap between these two ideas.

If there is something eternal and changeless and separable, knowledge of it clearly belongs to a theoretical science – not, however, to the study of nature nor to mathematics, but to a science prior to both. For the study of nature deals with things that exist separately but are not changeless, while parts of mathematics deal with things which are changeless but presumably do not exist separately but only as in matter. But the first science deals with things which both exist separately and are changeless . . .

There are therefore three kinds of theoretical philosophy: mathematical, natural and theological. (I call the study of the changeless and eternal 'theology' because this is obviously the category into which divine being falls.) Now the highest science must deal with the highest kind of thing. So, while the theoretical sciences are to be preferred over others, this – theology – is to be preferred over the other theoretical sciences.

One may raise the question whether first philosophy is universal or deals with just one kind of thing . . . Well, if there were no substance other than those formed by nature, natural science would be the first science; but if there is a changeless substance, knowledge of this must be prior and must be *first* philosophy – and universal just *because* it is first. And it will belong to it to consider being qua being, both what it is and the attributes that belong to it qua being. (*Metaphysics* E.1.1026a10)

Aristotle's attempt to bring together two different conceptions of first philosophy does not seem successful. God may indeed be the ultimate cause or explanation of all natural objects and changes; but it does not follow that knowledge of god will *include* knowledge of such objects and changes, or that theology will *itself* be concerned to study the attributes of being qua being.

General metaphysics

The part of the *Metaphysics* that deals with general metaphysics – as opposed to the small section concerned with theology – covers a vast range of topics. Here I shall say something about only two main questions: What are the basic realities of the world? and What makes them the things they are? These two questions will become a little clearer.

Reality and substance

We are surrounded by familiar changing objects – animals, plants, tables and clouds. Are these individual changing things the fundamental realities on which everything else depends? There are various ways in which this vague question might be taken, and various ways in which it might be answered negatively. It might, for instance, be suggested that not *all* ordinary changing things qualify as fundamental – our ontology need not be so hospitable. Some things can, as it were, be explained away; they are 'reducible'. If a cloud is just an agglomeration of water-particles our inventory of the basic items in the world need not include clouds as well as water-particles; and if a table is a construct from planks and nails our inventory need not include tables as well as planks and nails. It is easy to see how these commonsense examples could be taken further. Among Aristotle's predecessors the atomists had indeed claimed that all common objects are nothing but ephemeral compounds, and that it is atoms alone – atoms of various shapes and sizes – that are the permanent realities whose existence and movements explain everything in the world.

An alternative move – Plato's – had been not to the sub-sensible (atoms too small to be perceived) but to the super-sensible, the world of changeless Forms. The things around us are unreliable and illusory in various ways, impermanent clusters of appearances. Only changeless, intelligible universals (Justice, Equality etc.) can be the subjects of statements that are certainly true and can be relied on to remain true. This world's phenomena are intelligible only as copies or reflections of the Forms. Platonism finds basic reality not in the material constituents of ordinary objects, but in the universals which such objects imperfectly instantiate.

Now for Aristotle. In the *Categories* he distinguished substances (*ousiai*) from qualities, relations etc., and insisted on the priority of substances: qualities etc. can exist only as *characteristics of* substances. Within substances he distinguished primary substances (individual things – this man, this ship) from secondary substances (the species and genera of primary substances – man, ship); and he insisted on the priority of primary substances: species and genera have no independent existence, they are just *sorts of* primary substance. Individual things, therefore, are the basic items on whose existence everything else depends.

But what exactly are to count as individual things? In the *Categories* Aristotle mainly works with examples; but he does make one very important general point: one and the same primary substance is capable of receiving contraries. An individual man, say, can be hot at one time and cold at another: he is a *reidentifiable subject of change* (compare page 31). But do all such 'continuants' have an equal claim to go into a list of basic realities? Suppose that my neighbour is a tailor and a father. I can identify and reidentify 'this man' and 'this tailor' and 'this father'. But does the world contain a man *and* a tailor *and* a father? Does my drawer contain not only a hammer but also a handle and a head? Clearly not all continuants are equally fundamental. The term 'tailor' could easily be dispensed with; it is a mere abbreviation for 'man who makes clothes'. So what are the *basic* continuants, the really *primary* substances?

In the *Metaphysics* Aristotle limits the list of substances in several ways. (i) He rules out stuffs or materials – earth, gold, blood etc. Of course there really is gold in the world, and gold has its own distinctive character; but gold is not an individual thing, but 'more like a heap'. (As we say, 'gold' is a mass-term, not a count-noun.) (ii) Certain objects, though countable, are by their very nature dependent – hands, for example. There are hands only in so far as there are bodies with hands. Although hands are separable from bodies in a way – as colours or shapes are not – a separated hand in only an ex-hand. What it is to be a hand can be explained only by reference to the hand's role and function in a body. (iii) The powers and behaviour of artefacts are completely deducible from those of their natural constituents. Given the nature of wood, iron etc., it is in principle quite predictable how a certain construction of wood, iron etc. will perform. So there is no need to include artefacts in a list of the *basic* items in the world. (iv) Certain count-nouns standing for objects which are neither artefacts nor mere parts of natural objects can nevertheless be excluded from a basic vocabulary, since they can be defined away: a hero is a man who is brave, and if we have 'man' and 'bravery' in our inventory of what there is, we can leave 'hero' out. (Similarly for 'tailor', 'parent', and 'king'.) There are several reasons why the line between basic terms and dispensable ones should be drawn where it is drawn, but the most important point for Aristotle is that 'man' names a real biological species. In his favourite formula, 'man begets man'. There is no doubt an element of convention and convenience in our choice of classificatory words – we could have 'carved up reality' differently. But it is not a matter of convention or convenience that a male and female human being regularly procreate a (male or female) human being, while a male and female tailor do not regularly procreate a tailor.

It is, therefore, individuals belonging to natural kinds that Aristotle recognises as fully substantial – living things of all species. Such things have not only a nature of their own, but also the power to sustain and reproduce themelves (this being the basic *psyche*-power which defines the living, whether plant or animal: see page 56). Several types of consideration help Aristotle towards the view that individual plants and animals are the basic items in the world, not least his devotion to teleological explanation – his conviction that the higher and more complex explains the lower and simpler, not vice versa (see pages 41–54).

Matter, form, and essence

If Xs are individual substances, what *explains* their substantiality and their being the different individuals they are? It might seem that it is difference in matter or material constitution – what they are made of – that explains our being able to recognise and count different individuals. Two chairs may have exactly the same shape but they must be made from different bits of wood; and that is what makes them different chairs.

> The whole thing – such and such a form in this flesh and these bones – is Callias or Socrates. They are different because of their matter, which is different; but they are the same in form – for their form is indivisible. (*Metaphysics* Z.8.1034a5)

Yet to count Callias and Socrates as *two* depends on counting them as men, and to speak of them as *men* is to refer to their form.

'What makes Callias Callias?' 'Why is a man a man?' Such questions, as they stand, make no sense. Aristotle argues that the question must really be why such and such materials are (say) a man; and that the answer must give the form which such material constituents must have if they are to constitute (say) a man. Only of a composite thing (form plus matter) can the question 'What makes it a so-and-so?' be asked, and always in the sense 'What makes such and such matter a so-and-so?' The answer will be an account of the form (shape, structure or function) that defines so-and-so's. (The same general idea applies to non-substances. 'Why is there thunder?' must be taken as meaning 'Why is there noise in the clouds?' and answered by giving the efficient cause which explains noise in clouds and serves to define thunder. See pages 99–100 above.) It is only as so-and-so's that objects can be picked out and counted, and to be a so-and-so is to be a composite, matter with a certain form. It is qua having the form that the matter is a so-and-so; possession of the form explains the thing's being the individual substance it is.

> Since substance is a principle or cause, let us pursue it from this point of view. The question 'Why?' always amounts to this: 'Why does one thing belong to some other thing?' For to ask why the musical man is a musical man is to ask why the man is musical. To ask *why* a thing *is itself* is no question at all. (*That* the thing *is* must already be clear. That a thing '*is itself*' is a single answer to cover all cases – why a man is a man, a musician a musician, etc.; it applies to everything, a very quick

and easy answer!) [To say of anything that it 'is itself' is uninforma-tive, and to ask *why* it is itself is to ask a non-question.] We *can*, however, ask why a man is an animal of such-and-such a kind. Now we are evidently *not* asking why he who is a man is a man. We are asking, therefore, why something predicated of something belongs to it ... 'Why does it thunder?' That means: 'Why does noise occur in the clouds?' Thus the question is about one thing's being predicated of another. 'Why are these things – bricks and stones – a house?' Obviously we are asking the cause, i.e. (to speak abstractly) the essence. In some cases it is what the thing is for, as perhaps with a house or a bed, in some cases it is the first mover, since this too is a cause. [A house is defined by its function, thunder by its efficient cause.] ... When one term is not predicated of another it is not easy to see what is really being asked ... One must articulate the question properly – otherwise it is on the borderline between being a genuine question and not being a question at all. Since the thing's existence must be taken for granted, the question is clearly *why* the matter is a so-and-so. 'Why are these materials a house?' 'Because the essence of a house – what being a house is – is present' ... So what we seek is the cause, i.e. the form by reason of which the matter is a so-and-so; and this is the thing's substance. (*Metaphysics* Z.17.1041a9)

For various types of term the formal answer will vary. 'What makes rolls and coffee *breakfast*?' Their being consumed *in the morning*. 'What makes a plank a shelf?' How and where it has been fixed.

It remains to say what is the substance, in the sense of *actuality*, of sensible things [i.e. what makes certain matter, which is *potentially* a so-and-so, an *actual* so-and-so] ... There are obviously many differ-ences; some things are called what they are because of the way their matter is put together, e.g. things formed by blending, such as honey-water; others by being bound together, e.g. a bundle; others by being glued together, e.g. a boat; others by being nailed together, e.g. a box; and others in more than one of these ways. Other things are made what they are by position, e.g. a threshold and a lintel – since these differ by being positioned in a certain way; others by time, e.g. dinner and breakfast; others by place, e.g. the winds; and others by such perceptible qualities as hardness and softness, density and rarity, dryness and wetness – some things by some of these qualities, others by all of them, and in general some by excess and some by defect ... And the being of some things will be defined by *all* these features, because some parts of them are mixed, others blended, others bound together, others solidified, and so on with the other differences; for

instance, a hand or a foot [requires this kind of complex definition] . . .
Obviously, then, the actuality or formal definition is different for
different matter . . . [Aristotle now gives an example in which the
defining form is a function or purpose.] Those who seek to define a
house by saying that a house is stones, bricks and timbers are speaking
of the potential house, since these are the matter. But those who say it
is a container to shelter people and property, or something of that sort,
are speaking of the actuality. Those who combine both are speaking of
the third kind of substance, the composite of matter and form.
(*Metaphysics* H.2.1041b10)

The same priority of form is found when change is considered. The very
same plank or man gains and loses material continuously, and in a river
fresh water continually flows. But the form remains the same: to be the
same so-and-so as the so-and-so encountered last year it is necessary to be
a so-and-so, some material with that form, but not necessary to be made
of the *same* material.

On grounds such as these Aristotle holds in the *Metaphysics* that it is
form or essence (what it is to be a so-and-so), and not matter, that gives
identity and individuality to substances. Before making a final comment
on this I should like to give a few more quotations from *Metaphysics* Z,
partly to fill out points already made and partly to introduce further
ideas.

Substances are the primary things there are; other types of being
depend upon substantial being (Z.1).

There are several senses in which a thing may be said to 'be'. In one
sense the 'being' meant is 'what a thing is' or a 'this', while in another
sense it means a quality or a quantity or one of the other things that are
predicated as these are. While 'being' has all these senses, the primary
type of being is obviously the 'what', which indicates the substance of
the thing. For when we say of what quality something is, we say that it
is good or bad, not that it is six feet long or that it is a man; but when
we say *what* it is, we do not say 'white' or 'hot' or 'six feet long', but 'a
man' or 'a god'. All *other* things are said to be because they are
quantities of that which *is* in this primary sense, or qualities of it, or in
some other way characteristics of it . . .

Now there are several senses in which a thing may be called first; but
substance is first in every sense – in definition, in order of knowledge,
and in time . . . And indeed the age-old question which has always been
raised and puzzled about, what *being* is, is precisely the question, what
substance is. Some say there is really just one substance, others that
there are more than one – some holding that they are limited in

number, others that there are an unlimited number. We too therefore must concentrate chiefly primarily and almost exclusively on the question what it is that *is* in *this* sense. (*Metaphysics* Z.1.1028a10)

Does substantial being belong to *all* perceptible objects or only to some? Does it belong *only* to perceptible objects, or to other (intelligible) objects such as Platonic Forms (Z.2)? What *is* substantial being – what makes an object a substance? Of four suggested candidates, *matter* certainly fails. Since substances are the subjects of attributes, and qualities etc. exist only in them, it might seem that one gets to substance finally only when all characteristics are stripped away – i.e. when one gets, not just from pale tall man to man, but from man to absolutely indeterminate and characterless matter; but in fact this matter ('prime matter') must lack the individual, independent existence which is a key mark of substance (Z.3).

> The word 'substance' gets applied to at least four things; for the essence and the universal and the genus are all thought to be the substance of each thing, and so, fourthly, is the substratum [i.e. what underlies predicates and change]. Now the substratum is that of which every-thing else is predicated, while it is itself not predicated of anything else. So we must first determine the nature of this; for what underlies a thing has a strong claim to be its substance . . .
>
> We have now outlined the nature of substance, saying that it is that which is not predicated of a subject, but of which all else is predicated. But we cannot leave matters there. The statement itself is obscure, and further, on this view, *matter* becomes substance. For when all else is stripped off [to get to the substratum of which everything else is predicated] evidently nothing but matter remains. For the rest are characteristics, products and powers of bodies, or (like length, breadth and depth) quantities, and not substances; but the substance is rather that to which these *belong*. But when length and breadth and depth are taken away we see nothing left unless there is something that is bounded by these; so that on this line of thought matter alone must seem to be substance. By matter I mean that which in itself is neither a particular thing nor of a certain quantity nor with any other of the characteristics by which being is determined. For there is something of which each of these is predicated, whose being is different from that of each of the predicates (for the predicates other than substance are predicated of substance, while substance is predicated of matter). Therefore the ultimate substratum is of itself neither a particular thing nor of a particular quantity nor otherwise characterised.
>
> If we follow this line, then, matter proves to be substance. But this is

impossible; for both separability and 'thisness' are thought to belong chiefly to substance [characterless substrate lacks the independent individual existence of real substances]. And so form and the compound of form and matter would seem to be substance, rather than matter. (*Metaphysics* Z.3.1028b33)

Another candidate for the title of substance is *essence* (what it is to-be-X). Essence is what a thing is 'in itself', that on which its identity depends and a change in which would make it a different thing. Aristotle ties these ideas to the idea of definition – not the verbal definition of what a word means, but the definition of what something is; and he holds that only species of a genus will have an essence. 'Tailor' can have a verbal definition, but there is strictly speaking no essence of tailor, since a tailor does not become a different thing if he ceases to be a tailor. A tailor is a man who happens to do a certain job: he would become a different thing only if he ceased to be that *man* (Z.4).

> The essence of each thing is what it is said to be *in itself*. Being *you* is not being *musical*, since you are not in yourself (by your very nature) musical. It is what you are in yourself that is your essence. [Of *what* is there an essence? There could be a single word meaning 'pale man'. Let us suppose that 'cloak' means 'pale man'. Is there then an essence of cloak?]
>
> Is being-a-cloak an essence? Surely not. For the essence is precisely what something *is*; but when you have an attribute asserted of a subject other than itself, that is not precisely what some 'this' *is*; pale man is not precisely what some 'this' *is*, since thisness belongs only to substances. Therefore there is an essence only of those things whose formula is a definition. But there is a definition *not* wherever a word and a formula are identical in meaning, but where there is a formula of something *primary*; and primary things are those which do not involve one thing's being predicated of another. Nothing, then, which is not a species of a genus will have an *essence* . . . For everything else as well, if it has a name, there will be a formula giving its meaning ['cloak' means 'pale man'] (or instead of a simple formula we shall be able to give a more accurate one); but there will be no definition and no essence.
>
> Or is the term 'definition', like 'what a thing is', used in several ways? . . . In the primary and strict sense only substances have definition and essence, but other things have them also, only not in the primary sense . . . (*Metaphysics* Z.4.1029b13)

In a particularly difficult discussion in Z.6 Aristotle asks whether a thing is the same as its essence. In the case of accidental combinations like *pale man* it is *not* the same – for the essence of a pale man is being a man: if Callias is a pale man his remaining the same individual does not require him to remain pale, but it does require him to remain a man. What about man, then? If to be Callias is to be a man, is Callias *the same* as his essence, man?

In a later chapter (Z.13) Aristotle rejects the claim of the universal to be called substance.

> The universal also is thought by some to be in the fullest sense a cause, and a principle ... But it seems impossible that any universal term should be a substance. For the substance of each thing is what is peculiar to it and does not belong to anything else; but a universal is common – this is what we mean by 'a universal', that which is such as to belong to more than one thing. Of which individual then will this be the substance? Either of all or of none. But it cannot be the substance of all; and if it is to be the substance of one, this one will have to be the others also; for things whose substance is one and whose essence is one are themselves also one. (*Metaphysics* Z.13.1038b6)

Aristotle's general position then is this. It is individuals in real species that are basic substances (independent identifiable subjects of predication), and it is their essence or form that gives them this substantial being. So of the trio form, matter, compound, form is '*primary* substance', since it is the 'cause' of the substantial being of the compound.

There is much that is obscure and difficult in this. I pick out just one point. Why does not the claim of essence to count as primary substance fall victim to the argument Aristotle levels in Z.13 against the claim of universals? 'Things whose essence is one are themselves also one.' How can *man* be the essence of both Callias and Socrates, if Callias and Socrates are not themselves identical? There are two ways in which this difficulty may be tackled, and signs of both in Aristotle. First, allowing that in an ordinary sense the species *man* is a universal just as much as the genus *animal* is, one may nevertheless insist on its unique *connection* with the individual identity of Callias and of Socrates. Callias is not an individual who can first be picked out and then have 'man' predicated of him, manhood ascribed to him; his being an individual *is* his being a man, and his remaining the same individual is his remaining the same man. Only because he is a man is he an animal, and remaining the same animal *is*, for him, remaining the same man. (The same animal cannot be now a fox and now an ape.) Secondly, one may suggest that Aristotle does or should accept the idea of *individual* essences (so that *man* no longer counts as Callias's essence). There are several passages in which Aristotle uses the terms 'soul' and 'body' in discussing men and their essence. In these passages it is *soul* rather than *man* that appears as the individuating form of Callias – not his *species* but his *life*. Since 'soul' has a plural and often works like a count-noun, it is quite easy to suppose that Callias has one soul and Socrates another, and that these souls are individual essences.

I have only been able to give a highly selective and impressionistic view of Aristotle's general metaphysics. On many of his topics decisive progress has been made since his time; many others remain central to philosophical enquiry and continue to provoke controversy.

Theology: the existence and nature of God

'Proofs of God' are now somewhat unfashionable; but it is of historical interest to look at Aristotle's arguments, which held sway for so long. It is also of real philosophical interest to tease out his lines of thought and to decide which of his steps or assumptions are sound and which are doubtful or wrong.

A large part of the *Physics* develops an argument (quoted from on pages 21–3 above) that there must be an 'unmoved mover'. A long analysis of change and its presuppositions culminates in the conclusion that there must be a single, eternal, unchanging actuality to explain the eternal circular movement of the heavenly sphere and the existence of the world of change. In the *Metaphysics* Aristotle argues along the same lines.

It is necessary that there should be an eternal and unchanging substance. For substances are the first of existing things, and if they were all destructible, everything would be destructible. But it is impossible that movement should either have come into being or cease to be (for it must always have existed), or that time should. For there could not be a before and an after unless there were time. So movement is continuous in the same way as time is – time being either the same thing as movement or an attribute of it.

But now, if there is something that is *capable* of moving things or acting on them, but is not actually doing so, there will not *necessarily* be movement, since what has a power may not exercise it. Nothing, therefore, is gained by assuming eternal substances (like Plato's Forms) unless there is to be in them some principle capable of causing change; but even this is not enough ... For if it is not to *act*, there will be no movement. Moreover, even if it acts, this will not be enough, if its essence is potentiality. For there will not necessarily be eternal movement, since that which is potentially may possibly not be. There must therefore be an eternal principle whose essence is actuality. (*Metaphysics* Λ.6.1071b4)

Aristotle next says something more about the nature of the unmoved mover and about how it operates. (These further remarks explain his calling it 'God'.) It operates as a final cause, an object of thought and desire. Thus the heavenly bodies move in their eternal circular motion because they seek to be like the pure actuality of the unmoved mover, and such motion is the nearest they can approach to it.

This is how the object of desire and the object of thought cause movement: they move without themselves being moved . . .

The final cause, then, causes movement as being loved, but all other things cause movement by themselves being moved. Now if something is moved, it is capable of being otherwise than it is. So although the first movement [the continuous circular movement of the heavenly sphere] does exist in actuality, yet the sphere is, in so far as it is in movement, capable of being otherwise than it is – in place, even if not in substance. But since there is something which causes movement while itself unmoved, existing actually, this cannot in *any* way be otherwise than as it is. For movement in space is the first of the kinds of change, and movement in a circle the first kind of spatial movement; and this the first mover *causes* [and cannot be subject to].

The first mover, then, exists of necessity; *qua* necessary its being is good, and it is in this way [as good, i.e. as object of love and desire] that it is a principle. (*Metaphysics* Λ.7.1072a26)

Eternal and continuous change

A thesis at the centre of Aristotle's theological argument is this:

(T) There must be eternal and continuous change.

The proof of (T) is provided by the following:

(i) There cannot be a beginning or end of time;
(ii) Time is 'the number of change in respect of the before and after'.

The argument for (i) is that a 'now' is not a period of time, but a limit, cutting a period of time as a point cuts a line; a 'now' necessarily terminates one period of time and initiates another. It has time on both sides of it. So there could not be a first 'now' with no time before it, or a last 'now' with no time after it: there can be no beginning or ending of time. Aristotle's clear distinction between unextended points and extended lines, between durationless 'nows' and periods of time, was an achievement important for both philosophy and science. His claim that it is *incoherent* to suggest that there might be a moment before which (or after which) there was no time is evidently very plausible, and (i) is not at all easy to refute.

The argument for (ii) cannot be briefly stated. For Aristotle's definition or account of time is offered after other accounts and theories have been criticised and refuted, and it is itself expounded at some length. (What can be said is that Aristotle's discussion of time in *Physics* IV.10–14 is a masterly probe into a most tantalising topic; it is pure philosophising without any dogma or archaism.) The essence of (ii), as far as our present concern goes, is its claim that there can be time only because and when there is change, since time is a feature – or the measure, or something or other – *of* change. This claim is worth considering, even apart from the details of Aristotle's own account of time. If we can tell that time has passed only be noticing change, does it make sense to suggest that a period of time might elapse without any change whatsoever occurring in it?

If (i) and (ii) together imply that there must always have been change going on, do they also imply (T), that there must be eternal *and continuous* change? What does this further requirement mean? It means that not merely must there always be some change or other going on, but there must be some change that is always going on. The eternal change asserted in (T) is not a matter of successive changes of different things, overlapping so that there is no gap; it is a change, continuous and without any stop, of *one thing*. This very strong interpretation of (T) is essential if the further argument to the unmoved mover is to succeed. But it is not at all clear that (i) and (ii) really *justify* the addition 'and continuous' in (T).

Aristotle may be guilty of a fallacy here. He may just be confusing two propositions which are actually very different: 'Necessarily there is always something changing' and 'Necessarily there is something always changing.' Perhaps, however, he thinks that the existence of some *one* eternally moving thing is indeed necessary to guarantee that there *must* be eternal change. He may suppose that 'There is an eternal *series* of changing things' would imply 'Change is eternal', but would not imply 'Change is necessarily eternal.' If no changing thing were eternal it would seem to be a contingent fact – if it were a fact – that they overlapped in such a way that there was always change going on. If what we want to understand is not just that there *is* always change, but that there *must* always be change, we need something more than a mere overlapping series, we need a single thing whose very nature it is to be in eternal change.

The 'eternal and continuous change' of (T) is of course identified by

Aristotle with the circular movement of the outer heavenly sphere. He has arguments to show that circular movement is the only *possible* eternally continuous movement, and he uses observation to confirm that there is in fact something (the sphere of the fixed stars) that fills the bill.

The first unmoved mover

If we think of the history of the universe as a series of events, the earlier ones causing the later ones, it is tempting to ask 'What set it off, what was the *first* cause?' Aristotle of course is not concerned with this sort of 'first' cause, since he has argued that the history of the universe has *no* beginning in time – there was *no* temporally first event. The explanation he seeks is not, therefore, an efficient cause. There can be no efficient-cause explanation of why the sphere of the fixed stars has been in continuous circular movement *always*. There is however another type of explanation available, a type familiar to us from our experience of human action, namely an explanation that refers to desire and thought. My desires and thoughts explain my body's intentional movements, and are themselves explained by reference to the *objects* of desire and thought, objects which do not themselves change in being thought of and desired. Here then, in the explanation of a human action, we get back to an *un*moved mover, the object of the agent's desire. This is a final-cause explanation; and such an explanation (since it does not refer to some event preceding what is to be explained) *can* be offered for the eternal and continuous change of the sphere of the fixed stars. If this sphere is alive, and is capable of thought and desire, its continuous movement can be explained as due to a desire to approximate as closely as possible to some object of thought and desire. *This* will be the 'first unmoved mover', acting on the outer sphere in so far as it is loved and emulated by it.

Postponing for a moment further enquiry into the nature of the first unmoved mover, we can say that Aristotle's argument depends upon the assumptions that there must be an explanation for any change, and that for an eternal and continuous change the only available type of explanation is the final-cause type of explanation familiar and useful in talk of intentional movements. Among many questions and objections that may be raised I mention three. (i) we may be right to look for an explanation for every change, but can we be sure that there *is* one? If not, does not Aristotle's theology rest on pious hope? Against this Aristotle might reply that science too is based on assumptions or postulates – that events are law-governed and that nature is uniform. It is not therefore open to a scientist to complain that a theologian is guilty of pious hope in assuming that things are intelligible. Of course the individual beliefs of the scientist are open to checking and falsification in a way in which the theologian's beliefs are not. But that is because the theologian is trying to explain not some particular events that might have been otherwise, but the one continuous and eternal movement that could not have been otherwise. He is not asking 'What would explain this or that event?' but 'What could explain the necessity of the stars' eternal movement?' He cannot test his answer by seeing whether it works at other times, since it is offered in explanation of something that happens at all times (and that *must* so happen, given the argument about time and change).

(ii) It may be questioned whether the transference of the final-cause explanation from human action, or more generally animal movement, to the heavenly sphere is legitimate. After all, we understand the explanation in terms of thought and desire only in the context of people and animals going after particular objectives. Moreover in these cases we combine a final-cause explanation with an explanation of a straightforward physiological kind. When the dog wants the bone and runs for it, the bone (or the eating of it) is the final cause which explains his running; but the preceding seeing of the bone and the consequential changes in the animal's body constitute another and complementary explanation. So from the fact that we operate successfully with teleological concepts and explanations in this familiar area it does not follow that we can use them with understanding or safety in an utterly different area. The analogy between a dog's running for a bone and the heavenly sphere's eternal movement is (to say the least) only a partial one. On the other hand, where nothing *better* than a partial analogy can be found – for in discussing god or the universe we are inevitably discussing what is unique and not just one thing among others – may we not be forgiven for relying on it?

(iii) Let us grant for the sake of argument that we can understand why the fixed stars move as they do only by supposing that they move because of a desire they have, a desire to come as close as they can, in their 'life', to some higher form of life that they think of and love. Does this explanation imply that there must actually *be* that higher form of life? Perhaps somebody's splendid way of life is to be explained by his admiration and emulation for King Arthur or for Robin Hood. They are objects of thought, they are his ideals. But it does not follow that they really existed. You cannot have merely imaginary things or events as *efficient* causes: if *x* was efficiently-caused by *y*, *y* must have existed. But if *x* was finally-caused by *y*, all that must have existed is the thought of *y* and the desire for *y*, and these could have existed without *y*'s existing.

God and the world

If there is a first unmoved mover, what can be said about its nature?

Immune from change, and hence from matter, it must be pure actuality with no kind of potentiality. Aristotle's candidate for an activity that involves no change is pure thought – contemplation, not problem-solving. This is the life he ascribes to the first unmoved mover, who may now be called God. God is eternally engaged in *theoria* (an activity men enjoy only occasionally), and is eternally and supremely happy. What does God think about? In a rather mysterious phrase Aristotle says that since pure thought is the highest form of activity, and the divine being would not think of anything lower than the best, his thought must be 'thought *of* thought'. This should not be taken to mean that God thinks about his own thinking. The point is, rather, that in pure thought there is no distinction between thought and object of thought; God's eternal thinking cannot be distinguished from the eternal being of all the objects of his thought. This remains a baffling idea, related no doubt to the equally brief and difficult remarks about pure intellect in the *De anima* (see page 62 above).

Aristotle's God does not think about, or care about, this world of change. Yet its harmony and good order ultimately depends on him, since it results from the way in which all things imitate him after their fashion.

> We must consider also in which of two ways the nature of the universe contains the good, the highest good, whether as something separate and by itself, or as the order of the parts. Probably in both ways, as an army does: its good is found both in its order and in its leader, though more in the latter, since he does not depend on the order but it depends on him. And all things are ordered together somehow (not all in the same way) – fishes, birds, plants. The world is not such that one thing has nothing to do with another, but they are connected. For all things are ordered together to one end, but it is as in a household, where the freemen are least at liberty to act at random – for them everything or nearly everything is already settled – whereas the slaves and animals make only a small contribution to the common good and for the most part live at random ... All things must at least come to be dissolved into their constituents [from which other things can then be made], and there are other functions similarly in which all things share for the good of the whole. (*Metaphysics* Λ.10.1075a11)

The stars emulate God's activity by their eternal movement; this brings about the change of seasons and all the consequential rhythms of life, and also the ceaseless interchange of the four elements. Animals and plants aim in a different way at eternal life: individuals die, but by processes of reproduction the species are maintained for ever.

The most natural act for any living thing that has developed normally ... is to produce another like itself (an animal producing an animal, a plant a plant), in order to partake as best it can in the eternal and divine. That is what all things strive for, everything they do naturally is for the sake of that ... Since it cannot share in the eternal and divine by going on continuously as one and the same living thing ... it shares in it in the only way it can. What persists and goes on is not the animal or plant itself, but something *like* itself – not the same individual but a member of the same species. (*De anima* II.4.415a26)

Finally, one kind of animal, man, has a divine element in him, *nous*. He can thus emulate God in a way not open to other things, since he can himself engage in pure thought (although only for brief periods). This 'imitation of God' is man's highest form of activity (see pages 138–9 below).

10 Ethics

What is the best sort of life for a man to lead, and what political arrangements are the best? These are questions Aristotle addresses in his ethical works and in the *Politics*. As usual it is not only his answers that have continuing philosophical interest, but also the arguments leading to them. And supporting the arguments there are probing analyses and acute discussions of many topics: action, character, virtue, pleasure, reason, justice, and so on. From this rich tapestry I shall pick out a few threads, concentrating on ethics rather than politics. I will first say something about Aristotle's treatment of the central practical question, and then examine his analytical work on action and responsibility.

How best to live

Aristotle has two lines of approach to this question. Firstly, there is the approach through *endoxa*, what people think. A correct theory here, as in other areas, must be consistent with, and explain, the *phenomena* – the '*phenomena*' in this case being facts about people's beliefs and attitudes (see page 114). So in the first book of the *Nicomachean Ethics* Aristotle brings to the fore various widely-supported candidates for the title 'best life for man' (the life of pleasure, the life of practical activity, the philosopher's life); and he draws attention to characteristics that everyone would look for in the ideal life (it should be entirely satisfying, incapable of improvement, not subject to upset by external misfortunes). His discussion of this material brings out in a preliminary way some of the complexity of the issue. A man is a highly complicated animal with a variety of needs and aims, some of which are subordinate to others. A life-ideal will be a complex goal, not a simple one; it will have some kind of structure. So it is not enough to say, as one might have been tempted to, that the very best life will contain all the things generally recognised as desirable, notably pleasure and practical activity and thought. This would be a very superficial treatment of the *endoxa*. We need to ask *why* each of those things has a claim to enter into the best human life; to distinguish different *types* of pleasure, of activity, and of thought; to enquire how the various goods are to be weighed against one another when conflicts arise.

The elements that go into the best life may be expected to play different roles, just as in cake some ingredients may provide the bulk, others the flavour, while others again may serve simply as binding-agents. To say that the best life is pleasure and action and thought would be rather like saying that the best cake is butter and sugar and flour: true, perhaps, but not really a recipe. Now Aristotle is not – of course – going to be able to give a detailed recipe for making a good life. That it is not possible to do so is a point he himself stresses. How best to live is emphatically not a scientific or technical question with a precise, correct answer. Nevertheless he does say a great deal in the *Ethics* that helps to clarify the interrelations and interdependency of various aims and activities. Pleasure, for example, can be pleasure *taken in* action, and action can be *guided by* thought.

Aristotle's second line of approach is through the argument from man's 'function' or distinctive nature – see pages 14–16 above. The argument concludes that the best life is a life of excellent activity in accordance with reason. The rest of the *Nicomachean Ethics* seeks to fill in this very general formula, examining first the moral virtues (excellences of character) and then the intellectual virtues. Since reason operates in both the practical sphere and in the purely theoretical, one form of human activity that displays reason – as well as excellence of character – is good action; and one possible 'best life' would be a life of action, displaying practical wisdom and moral virtue. But another possible candidate would be a life of philosophical contemplation – reason employed in its non-practical role on unchanging subject-matter. I shall return later to the competition between these two rival lives.

Moral virtue and practical wisdom

'Virtue is a state of character that lies in a mean.' It is usually assumed that this thesis, Aristotle's 'doctrine of the mean', is a middle-of-the-road view of morality, and that he is advising us always to feel and act in a cautious and moderate way (Horace's 'golden mediocrity'). But this is a misunderstanding. For Aristotle does not say that every good *action* is intermediate – so that one should never, for example, give away *all* one had. It is the *virtue*, the state of character, that is, according to him, intermediate. This is because the kinds of action or feeling associated with the various virtues are actions and feelings capable of being in certain circumstances *over*done (or *under*done). Thus, generosity has to do with giving. The virtue of generosity does not require – or even allow

– that one should give away all one has to everyone on all occasions; giving can be excessive and inappropriate. The right state of character is that from which on each occasion the appropriate feeling and action results. On some particular occasion the appropriate action or feeling may be 'extreme' – all or nothing.

It must be admitted that some virtues fit more easily into Aristotle's pattern than others: generosity falls between meanness and prodigality, but are there two opposite vices between which kindness lies? Where this pattern does apply, it does not necessarily involve a dull or cautious view of virtue. In itself the doctrine of the mean does not imply anything as to *whereabouts* on the continuum from too much to too little the right point lies. We can all agree easily enough that the generous comes between the prodigal and the mean, but we may disagree entirely on where to draw the line: you may count as of generous character one whom I would regard as on the stingy side. For this reason the statement that a moral virtue is a state of character lying between two opposed bad states gives almost no practical guidance, whether of a conservative or of a revolutionary kind. The real colour and content of Aristotle's morality comes out not in his theoretical remarks, but in his detailed descriptions of individual virtues and vices; and in these he more or less adopts the ideas and attitudes of his contemporaries.

Another important thesis about moral virtues, a thesis inherited from Socrates, is that they go together – if you have one you have them all. This idea of the 'unity of virtue' is at first sight very strange. In real life people have some virtues and not others. However, this is because in real life we are not dealing with *perfect* examples of any virtue; to call a man 'brave' is not to imply that he could be guaranteed to display bravery on every conceivable occasion. If, for theoretical purposes, we are to explain what would be involved in the perfect possession of any one virtue, we find that we cannot allow defects anywhere in the character: all desires and feelings and tendencies must have been brought (by training) into a proper balance. For otherwise a defect in one area would always be liable to interfere with the proper operation of a virtue elsewhere. A greedy man cannot be reliably and completely honest, since his greed is bound in certain circumstances to be in conflict with his honesty. A coward cannot be 100 per cent generous or kind, since in certain circumstances cowardly fear will be bound to inhibit his generous or kind impulses. Thus at the level of theoretical analysis, if one is talking about ideal moral virtues, the thesis that they necessarily go together can be defended. And at the practical level it does have something important to teach us. It is a reminder of the tragic fact that a person with many excellent qualities can do terrible things and cause immense suffering because of a fatal flaw somewhere else in his character. So one should aim at achieving a certain balance and harmony among one's various desires and feelings, and not let any of them become much too strong or much too weak, lest this should have disastrous consequences for one's whole life.

Moral virtue, according to Aristotle, must be combined with practical wisdom (*phronesis*), the virtue of practical reasoning. This enables a man to decide on each particular occasion what would be fair or kind or generous – what would be the right thing to do. The excellence of his character then guarantees that he does it. But *how* does Aristotle suppose that the *phronimos* (the man of practical wisdom) decides on the appropriate thing to do? Does he calculate the possible consequences of alternative courses of action, or does he apply certain general rules? What is his final test or criterion of right action? If we want practical guidance about what to do in a difficult situation, Aristotle sensibly recommends us to ask a good and wise man for his advice. Such a man can often 'see' what is the best thing to do in the circumstances, without necessarily being able to explain why it is best. The moral philosopher, however, has an obligation to state what the aim or goal or criterion is, to which the *phronimos* looks in thinking out what should be done. Aristotle recognises that he has this obligation, but it is not clear that he fulfils it. It is tempting to suggest that since everyone values and seeks *eudaimonia* or well-being (for himself, his family, his friends), it is the promoting of *eudaimonia* that is the final objective of morality and the ultimate criterion of right action. However, if good and wise action is what *eudaimonia* partly consists in, we cannot explain *why* a certain way of acting is good and wise by saying that it promotes *eudaimonia*. I return to this question in a moment.

Philosophical contemplation

Aristotle does not have much to say in the *Ethics* about the subject-matter of pure philosophical contemplation (*theoria*), but he does argue that this is the highest and best activity of which a man is capable. Its objects are eternal and unchanging – so different from the muddle of change and chance with which we are concerned when we act in this world; and it is an activity that can reasonably be attributed to God himself – unlike such practical activities as giving donations and fighting battles. A life of *theoria* is above the human level, but Aristotle rejects with almost Platonic fervour the suggestion that a man should stay at the modest level of ordinary human affairs and not even try to spread his wings.

Such a life would be beyond a man. For it is not as being a man that he will live in that way, but in so far as something divine is present in him;

and as this divine element [*nous*] is superior to our composite human nature, so its activity [*theoria*] is superior to activity displaying the other sort of excellence [i.e. good action]. If reason is divine, then, in comparison with man, the life of reason is divine in comparison with human life.

Yet we must not – as some advise – think just of human things because we are human, and of mortal things because we are mortal. Rather we must, as far as we can, make ourselves immortal, and we must do everything possible to live in accordance with the best thing in us [*nous*]. For however small in bulk it may be, in power and value it surpasses everything.

Indeed this would seem actually to *be* each man, in that it is the authoritative and better part of him. So it would be strange if he were to choose not the life of his own self, but that of something else. What we said before will apply now: everything finds best and pleasantest what is truly its own. For men, therefore, the life of reason is the best and pleasantest (since reason more than anything else is man) – and consequently the happiest also. (*Nicomachean Ethics* X.7.1177b26)

There is a striking tension between the line of thought which leads Aristotle to praise and commend the life of practical virtue, and that which persuades him that *theoria* is man's best activity. The *ergon* argument (pages 14–16 above) invites us to discover a man's excellence and hence his good by noting what is characteristic and peculiar to man; and that is in fact *practical* reason. But the above passage tells us instead to identify ourselves with a *divine* element or power we have, and as far as possible to pursue an activity that is not in fact peculiar to man, but shared with God. We can recognise here a familiar conflict between two types of ideal: the ideal of a harmonious but decidedly human form of life as against a 'higher' ideal (whether ascetic or religious or intellectual) of an altogether more demanding kind.

The final recipe

So what in the end does Aristotle recommend as the best life for a man? Clearly nobody could actually survive without devoting some time and effort to activities other than *theoria*. But is Aristotle advising us to spend as little time and effort on other things as possible, and to attach no importance to any practical or moral concerns or claims in comparison with the value of theoretic activity? Should we, ideally, neglect our friends and family and community, and concentrate on our private intellectual life? It is not to be supposed that Aristotle would make so eccentric a recommendation, but it is not easy to explain how the claims of man-in-action and man-at-thought are in principle to be reconciled. (The problem can be widened and made more vivid for us if we extend the notion of *theoria* to cover intellectual and artistic activities other than philosophical contemplation. What shall we say of the artist who neglects his civic and family duties to produce masterpieces of painting?)

One tempting (commonsense) idea would be: first meet the needs of the moral life and thereafter concentrate on *theoria*. But are the claims of morality so limited that one *can* meet them to the full and still have time left over? No doubt minimal moral requirements do not amount to much, but what of the man who is truly kind, brave, generous, and so on – will he not be hard at work most of the time? It is no doubt true that even from the point of view of his moral achievement he needs 'time off', time for recuperative relaxation or play. But this has value only as preparation for further practical activity, and it cannot be identified with the divine *theoria* whose place in the best life we are trying to discover. Again, if *theoria* is indeed the highest activity, why should the needs of the moral life take any kind of precedence? For after all, in speaking of the moral life one is not speaking just of practical activities sufficient to keep one alive and fit to pursue *theoria*. One is speaking of time-consuming activities concerned with the welfare of others as well as the survival of oneself; one may even be called on to give one's life for the city. Why *should* such displays of practical virtue be given any priority over philosophic contemplation?

Aristotle does not himself deal with these questions, and I cannot here discuss the attempts that have been made to answer them for him. I will, however, mention one suggestion, designed to connect morality to contemplation, and so to prevent good action and *theoria* from seeming to be just unrelated and rival activities. The suggestion is that the very aim of morality is the promotion of *theoria*, that what makes a type of action count as good is precisely its tendency to promote *theoria*. On this view the ultimate justification for requiring and praising the sorts of acts and attitudes characteristic of the good man is that general adherence to the rules and standards he subscribes to would – in the long run and over all – maximise the amount of *theoria* possible in the community.

If this is so, then of course there cannot, at bottom, be any *conflict* between morality and philosophy, morality being in essence the system of conduct that favours and promotes philosophy. This suggestion also has the merit of supplying an answer to the question left unanswered above (on page 138): How does the *phronimos* decide what ought to be done – by reference to what ultimate good or goal?

The idea that morality is directed to promoting *theoria* may seem a bizarre idea, but when properly understood it is neither bizarre nor un-Aristotelian. It is important to notice at once that it is a theory about moral principles or types of action, not about particular acts. On individual occasions one does not ask what one can do to promote *theoria*; one applies moral rules ('keep promises', 'tell the truth') or puts into practice moral virtues (courage, kindness). But, the theory says, these rules and virtues are what they are, and can be justified, *because* a society whose members generally live according to them will be a society in which philosophic contemplation has the best chance of flourishing; such a society will provide the best possible harmonious setting in which those with the capacity for *theoria* will be able to exercise it.

That, then, is the theory. But is it at all plausible? If we were to ask 'What rules of life, if adopted in a community, would promote maximum *theoria* in the long run [or, in more modern terms, would produce the most civilised and cultured society]', *would* our answer look anything like ordinary morality? Well, the answer would surely have to take into account the whole nature of the human beings in the community, and their diversity. Only rules of life that ensured a balanced satisfaction of many human needs and desires (selfish and altruistic) could bring about and maintain a stable, smoothly-running society capable of encouraging and sustaining Institutes of Higher Learning. It is widely held that the aim of morality is the balanced satisfaction in the long run of diverse human needs and desires. The theory that the *ultimate* objective of morality is the promotion of *theoria* is quite compatible with saying that its more *immediate* objective is that balanced satisfaction; the society that achieves the latter will be the society in which *theoria* has the best chance to flourish.

I must leave the reader to consider whether this idea has any merit, and to what extent it might help Aristotle over some of the difficulties mentioned earlier.

Philosophy of action

The philosophy of action holds a central place in ethics. Many of its topics are examined carefully by Aristotle, and his remarks still serve as starting-points for philosophical investigations and stimuli to new ideas. In what follows I shall briefly discuss his account of what action is, how practical reasoning works, and how action contrary to reason is possible (pages 142–9). I will then consider his analysis of the conditions of responsibility, and of the pleas by which wrongdoers seek to evade blame and punishment (pages 149–55).

Action

Words like 'act' and 'do' have wider and narrow uses, and so do their Greek equivalents. To get to the meaning of 'action' (*praxis*) that is central to moral philosophy we must distinguish (i) the movements of living things from those of inanimate things; (ii) the movements of animals (which possess the faculties of perception and desire) from those of plants; (iii) the movements of men (who have the faculty of thought as well as those of perception and desire) from those of other animals, (iv) those movements of men which are in the narrow sense actions (or 'doings') from those which are productions (or 'makings').

The distinction in (iii) marks men off from other animals because they are capable of rational choice (*prohairesis*). They have the power to conceive long-range objectives and to think out how to attain them. Only such beings, according to Aristotle, are capable of actions that are open to moral praise and blame.

The distinction in (iv), between an action or doing (*praxis*) and a production or making (*poiesis*), is less easy. Here is one of Aristotle's explanations.

> Practical thinking governs productive thinking. Everyone who makes something makes it for some end or purpose. What is *made* is not itself the final end, only what is *done* is that – for *doing well* is indeed an end and is what desire aims at. (*Nicomachean Ethics* VI.2.1139b1)

There is an obvious contrast between making something simply because one wants to use it subsequently, and doing something for its own sake. It is only because there are activities we think worth pursuing for their own sake that we think it worth spending time and trouble on making the tools or instruments necessary for those activities: if nobody wanted to play golf there would be no reason to make golf-clubs. 'Practical thinking *governs* productive thinking' – what we make depends on, and is explained by, what we want to do.

Aristotle holds that the actions with which ethics is concerned are not done to produce something, and are not to be appraised, as technical performances are, as skilful or unskilful. They are done and valued for their own sake. The good man acts bravely and honourably not to win a prize, for an ulterior motive, or in order to enable himself to live well later; but because he sees that to act so *is* to live well, and that is what he wants to do.

Aristotle's way of contrasting a doing and a making (a *praxis* and a *poiesis*) leaves something to be desired. For the doings with which morality is concerned – honourable, generous or kind actions which the good man does because they are honourable, generous or kind – may themselves *be* 'makings' in the most literal sense. In making a table I may *be* keeping a promise, i.e. acting honourably. My kind action may *be* making an omelette for an invalid. So one cannot divide performances up into those that are actions and those that are productions: one and the same performance can be both. Indeed it might be claimed that *all* actions are in a broad sense 'productions'; in acting we intervene in the world to produce some change – actions are directed to outcomes. A brave man is fighting in battle. He is doing so because he is brave and for no ulterior motive; but he is (of course) fighting *for victory*. How then are we to answer the question whether his fighting is a *poiesis*, an activity aimed at producing something (victory), or a *praxis*, an action undertaken and valued for its own sake (as being brave)? His fighting seems to be both. I shall refer to this problem again later (page 153).

Choice and deliberation

Let us now return to the statement that men are capable of rational choice (*prohairesis*). Aristotle shows that choosing is not simply a kind of thinking and is not simply a kind of desiring, but that it involves both. Here is the conclusion of his analysis:

> What is chosen is something in our power which is desired after deliberation. Choice, therefore, must be deliberate desire of something in our power. Having reached a judgement as a result of deliberation, we desire in accordance with our deliberation. (*Nicomachean Ethics* III.3.1113a9)

Aristotle relies here on an earlier discussion of deliberation. In this he first points out that we do not *deliberate* about things which cannot be brought about by our efforts – 'no Spartan deliberates about the best constitution for the Scythians' – although we can of course think about such questions and advise about them. Nor, he goes on, do we deliberate when answers are cut and dried: 'deliberation is concerned with things that usually happen in one way rather than the other, but where the outcome is not certain, or with things in which it is quite indeterminate'. Aristotle adds a further restriction:

> We do not deliberate about ends, but about means. A doctor does not deliberate whether to heal, nor an orator whether to persuade, nor a statesman whether to produce law and order; nor does anyone else deliberate about his end. They assume the end, and ask themselves how and by what means it can be attained. If it seems that it can be brought about in a variety of ways, they ask how it can be brought

about most easily and best. If it can be brought about by one means only, they ask how it is to be achieved by this means – by what means this is itself to be achieved – until they come to the first cause, which in the order of discovery comes last. [Deliberation ends when one has reached something one can oneself do to set the ball rolling, to initiate a series of changes that will bring about the desired outcome.] . . .

Deliberation is about what the agent himself is to do, and actions are for the sake of things other than themselves. Thus the end cannot be a subject of deliberation, but only the means to the end. Nor indeed can particular facts be a subject of deliberation, e.g. whether this is bread or has been properly baked – these are matters of perception. If a man always deliberates, it will go on to infinity. (*Nicomachean Ethics* III.3.1112b11)

Two main points need to be made about this. First, surely practical deliberation is not always an investigation to find means to an end, to discover the steps by which a desired result can be achieved? One may, for example, have to ask oneself what would be the honourable thing to do, and this is not a question about means to an end; or one may have to weigh up the pros and cons of alternative courses of action. As a criticism of Aristotle – for describing deliberation in terms of means and ends – this point is misdirected. For the Greek words rendered 'means to an end' mean literally 'things related to (or directed to) an end (or goal)', and the phrase can quite well be used in contexts where the notion of *instrumental* means to an end – of steps directed to a desired result – would be inappropriate. So what Aristotle says can accommodate the example mentioned above. In trying to decide what would be the honourable thing to do my end or aim is to do whatever is honourable, and I am wondering by what action I should achieve this. It is true that Aristotle's examples of deliberation in *Nicomachean Ethics* III are in fact instrumental means. But in books VI and VII examples of the other type are used: a man concludes that he should do a certain thing because it is a thing *of a certain kind* (honourable, kind etc.). It is clear that both these kinds of thinking are common in life. Both are often complicated by the interplay and possible conflict between different goals or principles. An action leading to one desired goal may prevent my achieving some other goal; the act that would be honest would also, alas, be unkind.

Secondly, is it correct to say that one cannot deliberate about *ends*? This need not imply that some objectives are absolutely immune from being deliberated about (and adopted or rejected), but only that any *particular* piece of deliberation must take *some* goals, aims or principles for granted. I cannot simultaneously deliberate how to make a fortune and whether to adopt wealth as an objective; and I can think about the latter question only on the basis of *some* aims or wishes or preferences I already have and am not now scrutinising.

But what about a man's fundamental aims, his idea of *eudaimonia*, the life most worth living? Does his conception of *eudaimonia* depend ultimately on his genetic make-up and his upbringing, or can he have reached it by some form of thinking? If one cannot deliberate about what would be the best life without making use of some criteria for putting one life ahead of another, how are the criteria themselves obtained? This question will come up again later as a problem about responsibility (page 154).

Acting against reason (akrasia)

Deliberation or practical reasoning should terminate in a rational choice and appropriate action. Deliberation enables a man to see what he must do if he is to achieve his objective. In the standard case he does it; if he does not, some explanation is called for. Failing to do what you know you should do, or doing what you know you should not do, is *akrasia* (see pages 12–14). The problem of *akrasia* exercised Socrates and Plato and is discussed at some length by Aristotle.

But why is it a *problem*? It may be regrettable that people are often akratic, but is it difficult to understand? There seem to be two questions for the philosopher: (i) How in detail is one to *describe* the situation of the akratic man? Does he at the moment he does x still and clearly know that x is a bad thing for him to do, and that something else, y, would be best for him to do? Or is this knowledge suppressed or blurred by the strongly present desire attracting him to x? It might seem rather important to decide whether one is speaking of a man who does what he knows to be *morally bad* or of a man who does what he knows to be *bad for him*. For it might well be thought unpuzzling (though deplorable) that a man should do what he knows to be morally bad, that he should be more concerned at the moment for his own welfare than for what is morally good – which often serves the welfare of others. If however the morally good and a man's own (real) good actually coincide, as Aristotle follows Socrates and Plato in fervently maintaining, then this unpuzzling case turns into the other and puzzling case: a man knowingly does what is bad for himself. Is it not absurd to suppose that anyone (who is not a maniac) should intentionally harm himself? Must we not say that at the moment of action he fails to realise the nature and consequences of what he is doing – so that he does *not* do what he now knows to be bad for him, but what he knew before (and will know later) to be bad for him? In this way we may try to conjure away the case in which a man, knowing that *this* is the best thing for him to do, nevertheless does *that*.

(ii) The akratic situation is common, and the akratic man is commonly criticised and censured. But is this justifiable? If some passion or temptation distorts or clouds a man's judgement, so that he wrongly supposes that he ought to do *x* (or at least may do *x*), he can hardly be blamed for doing *x*, for doing what he thinks he ought to do (or at least may do). If, on the other hand, passion moves him to do *x* even though he still recognises *x* to be a bad thing for him to do, is he not to be pitied rather than blamed, pitied as the victim of a force which he himself wishes he were unaffected by and which he even tries to resist?

Aristotle on akrasia

Aristotle asks whether or in what sense the akratic man 'knows' that what he is doing is bad. In his usual way he draws some important distinctions. First, knowledge may be dispositional or actualised. ('Tom knows the date of the battle of Waterloo.' But he may not be thinking about it at the moment. His knowledge is dispositional, not actualised; he is not at present using it.) There is nothing at all to be surprised at if a man acts against merely dispositional knowledge, knowledge which he *has but is not attending to*.

> We speak of *knowledge* in two ways: both a man who has knowledge but is not using it, and a man who is using knowledge, are said to know. So it will make a difference, when a man does what he ought not to do, whether he has but is not exercising the knowledge [that he ought not to do this], or whether he is exercising it. It is only the latter case that raises a problem. (*Nicomachean Ethics* VII.3.1146b31)

Next, it will not be surprising that a man acts against his own interest or principles if, through ignorance of some relevant fact, he fails to realise that the action *is* against his own interest or principles. However keen I am not to touch liquor, and however clearly I appreciate the damage it would do to me, I shall nevertheless drink liquor if you lace my coffee with whisky without my knowing it.

Aristotle next distinguishes two *types* or *stages* of merely dispositional knowledge. The man who is asleep or drunk or in a fit is one stage further removed from actualised knowledge than is a sober, sane, waking man. The sober man's knowledge of some matter can easily be actualised – you need only ask him the appropriate question. The drunk, on the other hand, must first be sobered up, and then asked the question.

> Within 'having knowledge but not using it' we can see a difference in the having, so that there is such a thing as having knowledge in a way

and yet not having it, as with someone who is asleep or mad or drunk. Now this is exactly the condition of a man under the influence of passions; for outbursts of anger and sexual desires and other such passions do actually alter our bodily condition, and sometimes even produce fits of madness. Clearly, then, akratic people are like people who are asleep or mad or drunk (*Nicomachean Ethics* VII.3.1147a11)

An akratic person may say 'What I am doing is wrong.' But that does not prove that he actually knows it to be wrong. Parrots, children and drunks often say things without in the least understanding (or, therefore, meaning) what they say.

That a man *says* knowledgeable things is no proof that he knows them. Men under the influence of these passions may utter scientific proofs or recite the poems of Empedocles, but they do not understand what they are saying. Beginners at a subject can put together the sentences, but they do not yet know the subject – it has to become part of themselves, and that takes time. We must therefore take what men say when they are acting akratically in the way we take what actors on the stage say. (*Nicomachean Ethics* VII.3.1147a18)

Aristotle now comes closer to the detail of an akratic situation.

One opinion is universal while the other is about the particular facts (which fall within the sphere of perception). When a single opinion results from the two, the conclusion reached is in one type of case [non-practical] necessarily *affirmed*, while where the opinions are concerned with bringing things about it must immediately be *done*. Thus, for instance, if 'Everything sweet ought to be tasted' and 'This is sweet' ('this' being some particular sweet thing), the man who can and is not prevented must at the same time [as he draws the obvious conclusion] actually do this [i.e. taste the sweet thing].

Now when a universal opinion is present in us forbidding us to taste, and there is also the opinion that 'Everything sweet is pleasant' and that 'This is sweet' (and this opinion is active), and when appetite happens to be present in us, the one opinion bids us avoid the object, but appetite leads us towards it – for appetite can move each of our bodily parts. So it turns out that a man behaves under the influence, in a way, of a principle and an opinion – and of one not contrary in itself, but only incidentally, to the right principle; for the appetite is contrary, not the opinion. (This is why the lower animals are not akratic: they have no power of universal judgement, but only imagination and memory of particulars.)

The explanation of how the akratic man's ignorance is dissolved, and how he regains his knowledge, is the same as that which applies to the drunken or sleeping person; it is not peculiar to the akratic condition. We must accept the physiologists' account of the matter. (*Nicomachean Ethics* VII.3.1147a25)

This account of the various 'opinions' in play in *akrasia* is not entirely clear, and two alternative interpretations suggest themselves. (i) The akratic man is well aware that X-things are bad and that this is an X-thing. But he fails to draw the conclusion, he fails to realise that this is bad, because there is present in him a strong desire for pleasant things and the knowledge that X-things are pleasant. His case can be represented thus:

X-things are bad	X-things are pleasant
This is an X-thing	
[This is bad]	This is pleasant

That this is bad he fails to recognise, even though it follows from premises of which he is aware. That this is pleasant he does realise, and consequently he does it (or takes it). (ii) Though well aware that X-things are bad, the akratic man fails to realise that this is an X-thing, and so (naturally enough) fails to realise that it is bad. He does however realise that this is an Y-thing; and knowing Y-things to be pleasant he realises that this is pleasant, and so goes for it. Thus:

X-things are bad	Y-things are pleasant
[This is an X-thing]	This is a Y-thing
[This is bad]	This is pleasant

In both (i) and (ii) the explanation for the square brackets – for the man's *failure to realise* something – is that he is under the influence of a strong desire for the pleasant, which prevents him thinking clearly. He is in a state like that of the drunken or sleeping man. He may utter the words 'This is bad', but he utters them without really grasping their significance, without really knowing that this is bad.

Aristotle does here explain how there can be cases of going against one's own principles which are not cases of doing what one realises at the moment of action to be wrong; and how the failure to see what is right and wrong now can be explained by the powerful effect of desire for the pleasant, a desire which often diverts our attention and leads us to suppress unwelcome thoughts. But surely this account cannot fit all cases of *akrasia*. Not everyone who says 'I know I should not be doing this' can plausibly be likened to a drunk or to a person in a frenzy. For there is also, unfortunately, the man who does wrong, or does what is bad for him, realising full well at the time that he is doing it. Aristotle is anxious to maintain some sort of necessary connection between thinking something the best thing to do and doing it. Human behaviour is only intelligible because there is *normally* such a connection between judgement and action. But it is going too far to suggest that a man *always* does what he at the time thinks best – on individual occasions a special desire (e.g. for immediate pleasure) may break the connection between judgement and action.

The text I have been discussing does not contain all that Aristotle has to say about the nature of *akrasia*. In particular, he quite often speaks elsewhere in terms of a battle, a psychological conflict, rather than in terms of 'ignorance' or failure to realise what should be done. At one place he draws a useful distinction between two very different types of *akrasia*: weakness, where a man does not stick to the conclusion or decision he has reached, and impetuosity, where he does not stop to think at all. Neither of these types seems to fit exactly into the account outlined above. The truth is that action against one's own principles, aims or interests is a complicated phenomenon; no simple analysis can do justice to all the varieties of *akrasia*.

The second main question I mentioned, concerning the *culpability* of the akratic man, is really a part of the wider question whether blame and punishment can ever be justified. I shall return to this shortly.

Responsibility and excuses

The nature of human action is a large and complicated area of philosophy. The analysis of the conditions of responsibility and of the pleas by which blame for wrongdoing may be averted or mitigated presents a more limited task, and one in which Aristotle laid some secure foundations. A contemporary treatment, such as that in Austin's famous paper 'A Plea for Excuses', shows greater refinement and develops additional distinctions; but it proceeds much as Aristotle did – by appeal to current usage (both ordinary language and the language of the courts) and by discussion of cases and circumstances. I will first outline Aristotle's treatment (pages 149–52), and then touch on two deeper problems that his account – any such account – forces on our attention (pages 152–5).

Voluntary and involuntary

The basic distinction which Aristotle draws and elucidates is that between what is *hekousion* and what is *akousion*. These terms are usually, and conveniently, translated 'voluntary' and 'involuntary'. (Anyone sensitive to the normal very restricted use of these English adjectives will find it awkward to have them employed to draw the very comprehensive contrast made by Aristotle. For much of what he says the renderings 'intentional' and 'unintentional' would be preferable.) The key point is that the distinction is supposed to correspond to the distinction between what is and what is not liable (in principle) to be praised, blamed or punished. A man is held responsible only for what he has done *hekousiōs*, 'voluntarily'. Aristotle opens his discussion on this note:

> Virtue is concerned with feelings and actions; praise and blame are bestowed on voluntary ones, pardon (sometimes also pity) on involuntary ones. To define and distinguish the voluntary and the involuntary is, therefore, essential if one is enquiring into virtue – and useful for legislators too, in connection with the assigning of honours and punishments. (*Nicomachean Ethics* III.1.1109b30)

Aristotle proceeds to his central thesis: 'those things are accounted involuntary which take place by force or owing to ignorance'. To fill this out: things done are involuntary when the doer is forced by overwhelming physical constraint ('the moving principle [*arche*] is outside, nothing being contributed to it by the person who acts – or, rather, is acted upon'), or when he acts because of ignorance of relevant facts. Conversely, in a voluntary action 'the moving principle is in the agent himself, and he is aware of the particular circumstances of the action'.

Mixed actions

Aristotle has little to say about force, cases of sheer physical constraint, where indeed the very notion of an *agent* and of his performing an *action* is really out of place; but he discusses at some length the more interesting situations where threats or bribes or other pressure may influence an agent and may excuse, mitigate or even justify what he does. Take the ship's captain who throws his cargo overboard to prevent the loss of the ship and its crew in a storm. Nobody *wants* to throw a cargo overboard, yet in present circumstances the captain prefers this to a greater evil.

> Such actions, then, are *mixed*, but they are more like voluntary actions [than like involuntary ones]; for they are worth choosing at the time when they are done ... and 'voluntary' and 'involuntary' should be used with reference to the time of action ... Such actions, therefore, are voluntary, though in the abstract perhaps involuntary – since no one would choose any such act in itself. (*Nicomachean Ethics* III.1.1110a11)

Something unwelcome in itself may be acceptable and even welcome under special circumstances – if the only alternative is something much worse. Aristotle could have given a better and more refined account of such cases if he had made use of a larger range of adjectives and adverbs. It is such expressions as 'reluctantly' or 'under pressure' that bring out the complexity of the situation faced by the agent, indicating that he did not *want* to act so, though in the end he chose to. Aristotle is probably embarrassed in his treatment of 'mixed actions' by the fact that willingness is normally suggested by the Greek word *hekousion*. The captain surely throws out the cargo *un*willingly. Since we easily distinguish 'intentionally' and 'willingly', we find no difficulty in saying that the ship's captain jettisoned the cargo intentionally yet unwillingly. (An alternative approach involves distinguishing *different* actions, or action-descriptions, thus: The captain did two things, *he saved the ship and crew* and *he lost the cargo*; he saved the ship and crew very willingly, he lost the cargo very unwillingly.)

Ignorance

On ignorance Aristotle makes a number of important points: (i) he distinguishes ignorance of material facts from 'ignorance of the universal', i.e. of what in general is morally or legally requisite. People are required to know the law; and 'I didn't know one ought to be honest' is no excuse. (ii) Aristotle does not think that ignorance of fact always excuses. The agent may well be blamed for what he does in ignorance, if he himself is responsible for his being ignorant – if, for example, he got himself drunk or negligently failed to find out the facts.

> A person who is drunk or in a rage is not thought to act *because of* ignorance, but because of one of the causes mentioned – even though he does what he does *in* ignorance and not knowingly. (*Nicomachean Ethics* III.1.1110b25)

> We actually punish a man for being ignorant if he is thought to be responsible for the ignorance, as when penalties are doubled in the case of drunkenness. For the moving principle (*arche*) is in the man himself: he had the power not to get drunk, and his getting drunk was the cause of his ignorance. And we punish those who are ignorant of anything in the laws that they ought to know and that is not difficult, and so too with anything else that they are thought to be ignorant of through carelessness. It was, after all, in their power *not* to be ignorant, since they could have taken care. (*Nicomachean Ethics* III.5.1113b30)

(iii) Aristotle recognises the great variety of factors and circumstances of which an agent may be ignorant.

A man might mistake his son for an enemy ... or think that a pointed spear had a button on it... One might give someone a drink to save him, and actually kill him, or one might want just to touch someone, as in sparring, but really wound him. Ignorance may relate, then, to any of these matters, and the man who was ignorant of any of them is taken to have acted involuntarily, especially if he was ignorant on the most important points, the circumstances of the action and its consequences. (*Nicomachean Ethics* III.1.1111a11)

Aristotle's excellent discussion leaves a large number of problems untouched. I will mention just three. (*a*) That a man is blameworthy for the ignorance in which he committed an offence certainly prevents his denying all responsibility for what he did. But it is open to discussion exactly how he should be treated as regards moral appraisal and as regards legal penalties. Suppose that what he did in his drunken state caused others great loss and suffering. Because he was to blame he should certainly be made to compensate those who suffered. But we should not be tempted to call him a cruel man, nor would our courts punish him in the same way as they would if he had caused the loss and suffering intentionally. (*b*) The notion of being responsible for one's ignorance requires investigation. A man may do something, knowing perfectly well that it is bound to put him in a state of dangerous ignorance (e.g. stupefied drunkenness). But culpable *negligence* is not like that. Indeed Aristotle's whole account of the voluntary and involuntary fails to cover *omissions* – failures to act – though these are just as liable to blame and punishment as are actual misdeeds. (*c*) We may agree that a man can be to blame for killing his father even though he did not know it was his father, *if* he had culpably failed to find out. But we certainly cannot say that he killed his father voluntarily, nor could a Greek have said that this man did so *hekousiōs*. So the tie between the distinction *voluntary/ involuntary* and the distinction *liable to blame etc./not liable to blame etc.* is here cut or at least loosened.

The two 'deeper problems' that I promised to touch on concern the identity of actions, and the ultimate justification for holding people responsible for their voluntary actions.

The identity of actions

Any attempt to explain action and to elucidate the conditions of responsibility for actions must eventually grapple with the question what counts as an action. This innocent-looking question, about the *identity* of actions, is in fact a very difficult and complex one; but it is easy enough to indicate the general character of the problem. One would suppose, since one is constantly interested in people's actions, that it would be easy to say how *many* actions a person had performed in a given period. A moment's consideration shows that it is not at all easy – that it is not, indeed, clear that there *is* any answer to such a question. Yet how can we urge people to perform actions of one kind or another, or judge their character from their actions, if we cannot pick out, and in principle count, their actions in a given period of time? Now one reason for this difficulty is that a single 'big' action can be regarded as being made up of several 'small' actions: asked what I have done in the last five minutes I might say 'I've washed up' or I might say 'I've washed and dried the cups, I've scoured the frying-pan . . .'. (Part of an action is itself an action, just as part of a piece of cheese is a piece of cheese – whereas part of a sausage is not a sausage.) There is however a further difficulty about identifying and counting actions. What I do over a given period, or at a particular time, can itself seem to be two or more actions. I am not speaking of such a case as that in which a man simultaneously waves goodbye with one hand and shoots himself with the other, but of the fact that *each* of these two performances can be seen as more than one action. Thus the waving goodbye was 'also' moving his hand (and 'also' perhaps frightening the cat); and in shooting himself he was also making a loud noise – and perhaps waking the neighbours too.

These last examples bring out a point of the greatest importance for ethics, and for the law. What I did at a certain time may expose me to several different criticisms or accusations, and I may have different answers to offer to them. Thus I may say that I *shot myself* deliberately, because in my desperation I wanted to die; I *made a loud noise* knowingly but not because I actually wanted to (indeed I was reluctant to make such a noise); I *woke the neighbours* without realising it, quite unknowingly. To take a more serious case, a case that Aristotle uses in his discussion of the voluntary or involuntary. Oedipus killed his father when provoked by him at a chance meeting; he did not realise it was his father, nor did he intend actually to *kill* the man he hit. Thus he *hit the man* intentionally, under provocation; he *killed the man* unintentionally, by accident; he *hit and killed his father* unknowingly, and hence, of course, unintentionally.

How is a theory of action to cover and explain these facts? It may be suggested that one and the same action can be described in various ways and can receive various kinds of praise, blame, criticism – in short, appraisal – under its various descriptions. Alternatively, each description of a given bodily movement may be taken to pick out a different action. Both views have their difficulties and raise complicated problems. Aristotle himself does not confront this problem in general (though he does in the *Physics* investigate what is to count as a single *change* or *movement*). But what he says brings it very much to the fore, and his failure to clarify it shows itself in the difficulty we found (pages 142–3) in his distinction between action (*praxis*) and production (*poiesis*). Is the difference between an action and a production a difference in *what* is done, or is it just a matter of how a given performance is described and appraised?

Responsibility

However the difficulties just discussed are to be dealt with, it is clear that an essential element in the analysis of action is the operation of an 'internal principle'. Every natural object has an internal principle of change (page 34); what distinguishes human action is that here the internal principle is desire in some form (*choice*, in the fully-fledged deliberated action). *What* exactly desire is, and how this psychological concept is related to physical concepts and processes, are questions (as Aristotle would say) for another enquiry. But what does concern ethics is this: Why should the fact that my action results from my desire justify my being punished for wrongdoing, if I am *not* responsible for my desire? Surely my desires simply reflect the sort of person I am; and being that sort of person I cannot help desiring what I do desire – and hence, acting as I do act.

Aristotle addresses himself to this challenge in *Nicomachean Ethics* III.5. One point he insists on, quite rightly, is that liability to blame and liability to praise go together: one cannot excuse one's bad behaviour on the ground that one is 'that sort of person', and yet still claim praise for one's good behaviour. He also makes the important practical point, that blame and punishment are deemed appropriate only where they can, by acting on a person's desires, effect changes in his conduct. But on the deeper issue of the justification – as opposed to the efficacy – of blame and punishment he seems less happy. He argues that since it is by doing good or bad actions voluntarily that we come to have virtues or vices, the latter are themselves voluntary and we can therefore be praised or blamed for them – even though it is not now open to us to decide to change our characters. Character traits are built up by corresponding behaviour – any fool knows that if you keep behaving in a certain way you will develop a settled habit or disposition to behave in that way; and we can certainly be blamed for the foreseen results of our voluntary actions. This argument hardly meets the case. Suppose that a person was from the start and by nature attracted to evil, or that he was as a child brought up in bad ways: is *he* to blame for his genetic make-up or childhood upbringing? Might not every bad man claim with some plausibility that his present deplorable condition of character is the result, if you trace it back far enough, of actions he did *before* he was old enough to know better – actions for which his inherited temperament and environmental influence must be held responsible?

It would be in harmony with Aristotle's general approach to say that just as men are, by nature, animals capable of speech and of reasoning and of choosing in the light of reasons, so they are, by nature, animals who (at a certain age) *accept* responsibility for their actions and hence are capable of being affected by praise and blame; as they grow up they *identify* themselves with their main aims and desires – and do *not* look upon these as things handed over to them (by inheritance and training), things for which they themselves cannot be held responsible. Perhaps no *further* justification can be given for holding people generally responsible for what they do than that they are – not plants or beasts but – people.

*

Aristotle's works have been studied closely and continuously for many centuries, and not only in the West. They have an importance in the history of civilisation which it is not easy to exaggerate; directly and indirectly they have exercised a quite remarkable influence on the development of philosophy, theology and science.

These works remain as fresh and enjoyable and thought-provoking as when they were written. I hope that the reader of this book will now be eager to look into some of them for himself.

Further Reading

General

Excellent general surveys of Aristotle's life and works are to be found in:

D. J. Allan: *The Philosophy of Aristotle* (2nd edition, Oxford, 1970),

G. E. R. Lloyd: *Aristotle* (Cambridge, 1968),

W. D. Ross: *Aristotle* (London, 1923).

Any of these will provide a valuable supplement to the present volume. Ross's book is the fullest and can serve as a very useful work of reference.

Translations

The standard translation into English is the 'Oxford Translation':

J. A. Smith and W. D. Ross (eds): *The Works of Aristotle translated into English* (Oxford, 1910–52).

A convenient one-volume abridgement of this is:

R. McKeon (ed.): *The Basic Works of Aristotle* (New York, 1941).

Nearly all of Aristotle's works are translated in the Loeb Library (published by Heinemann), with facing Greek text. The Clarendon Aristotle series (Oxford) contains translations of selected works with philosophical commentary. The translations in the Everyman series cannot be recommended.

Further reading

The best plan is first to read whole treatises (or at any rate long stretches) fairly briskly, and then to focus on particular passages or problems. In what follows I will give some advice on what texts to read. For guidance on modern books and articles I shall in the main refer to the extremely helpful bibliographies contained in four volumes which should be obtainable in, or through, any good library:

Articles on Aristotle, edited by J. Barnes, M. Schofield, R. Sorabji (London, 1975–9).

Ethics and politics

Among the most accessible of Aristotle's works, in subject and style, is the *Nicomachean Ethics*. Good translations are by W. D. Ross (Oxford Aristotle, vol. IX, reprinted with revisions in The World's Classics series), by H. Rackham (Loeb Library), and by H. Tredennick (Penguin Classics). To the articles and books mentioned in *Articles on Aristotle*, vol. 2, pp. 221–8, add:

A. O. Rorty (ed.): *Essays on Aristotle's Ethics* (Berkeley, 1980).

Aristotle's *Politics* has a rather complicated structure and some of its books are of a mainly historical interest. A good introduction is:

R. G. Mulgan: *Aristotle's Political Theory* (Oxford, 1977).

There are satisfactory translations by E. Barker (Oxford, 1946), by H. Rackham (Loeb Library), and by T. A. Sinclair (Penguin Classics). Books III–IV are translated, with philosophical comments, by R. Robinson (Clarendon Aristotle series, Oxford, 1962). For articles and books see *Articles on Aristotle*, vol. 2, pp. 228–33.

Logic and philosophy of science

Categories and *De interpretatione* are short, but important for both logic and metaphysics. They are translated, with notes, by J. L. Ackrill (Clarendon Aristotle series, Oxford, 1963).

The *Analytics* are difficult, especially for the Greekless reader, and it would be sensible to approach them after reading:

E. Kapp: *Greek Foundations of Traditional Logic* (New York, 1942),

W. C. and M. Kneale: *The Development of Logic* (Oxford, 1962), Chapter II,

W. D. Ross (ed.): *Aristotle's Prior and Posterior Analytics* (Oxford, 1949), Introduction.

The English translations of the *Prior Analytics* are not satisfactory; the Loeb is preferable to the Oxford translation. There is a very close translation of the *Posterior Analytics*, with notes, by J. Barnes (Clarendon Aristotle series, Oxford, 1975).

The *Topics* and *Sophistici elenchi* are best read in the Loeb translation by E. S. Forster.

Philosophy of mind

The basic texts are *De anima* (short, difficult, fascinating) and *Parva naturalia* (essays on such topics as sense-perception, memory, dreaming). The Oxford translation (vol. III) is good; the Loeb is to be avoided. A Clarendon Aristotle volume by D. W. Hamlyn (Oxford, 1968) contains a translation, with notes, of *De anima* II–III. For articles and books see *Articles on Aristotle*, vol. 4, pp. 179–87.

Natural philosophy

Works on nature form the main bulk of Aristotle's treatises, and deal with a great variety of subjects. The best approach is probably to read all or part of the *Physics*. There are good translations by R. P. Hardie and R. K. Gaye (Oxford Aristotle, vol. II), and by P. Wicksteed and F. M. Cornford (Loeb Library). There is a translation of *Physics* I–II, with philosophical commentary, by W. Charlton (Clarendon Aristotle series, Oxford, 1970).

For the important biological works start with *De partibus animalium* ('On the Parts of Animals'), I. Of this there are good translations by W. Ogle (Oxford Aristotle, vol. V), by A. L. Peck (Loeb Library), and – with philosophical notes – by D. M. Balme (Clarendon Aristotle series, Oxford, 1972).

For articles and books see *Articles on Aristotle*, vol. 1, pp. 199–205, and vol. 3, pp. 194–7.

Metaphysics

Aristotle's *Metaphysics* is in parts excessively difficult. It is best read in the translation by W. D. Ross (Oxford Aristotle, vol. VIII); and Ross's great edition (Oxford, 1924) contains very helpful chapter-by-chapter analyses. There are Clarendon Aristotle volumes containing books Γ, Δ, E (by C. A. Kirwan, Oxford, 1971) and books M, N (by J. Annas, Oxford, 1976). A guide to recent articles and books will be found in *Articles on Aristotle*, vol. 3, pp. 180–94.

Rhetoric and Aesthetics

The *Rhetoric* is not of great philosophical importance, though it contains some interesting material. Aristotle's *Poetics* was once very influential and is still well worth reading, perhaps with the aid of:

H. House: *Aristotle's Poetics* (London, 1956).

For articles and books see *Articles on Aristotle*, vol. 4, pp. 187–92.

Indexes

3 WORKS from which passages are quoted

More paperbacks from Oxford

The World's Classics

The Nicomachean Ethics

Aristotle

Translated with an Introduction by David Ross

In the *Nicomachean Ethics* (so called after their first editor,
Aristotle's son Nicomachus) Aristotle sets out to discover the good
life for man: the life of happiness or *eudaimonia*. Happiness for
Aristotle is the activity of the soul in accordance with virtue. Virtue
is shown in the deliberate choice of actions as part of a worked-out
plan of life, a plan which takes a middle course between excess and
deficiency. This is the famous doctrine of the golden mean –
courage, for example, is a mean between cowardice and rashness,
and justice between a man's getting more or less than his due. The
supreme happiness, according to Aristotle, is to be found in a life of
philosophical contemplation; but this is only possible for the few,
and a secondary kind of happiness is available in a virtuous life of
political activity and public magnificence.

The World's Classics

The Odyssey

Homer

This is the first English prose translation of the *Odyssey* to be
published for over thirty years. It is so successful that it will surely
take its place as one of the few really outstanding versions of
Homer's famous epic poem. Walter Shewring has with rare skill
reconciled the easy flow of the story with the formal uncolloquial
style in which it is told, and has perhaps come as close to the spirit
of the original Greek as our language allows.

'Walter Shewring is [a] scholar of great brilliance. . . He writes with
a tact, a formality and precision which are enviable and rare. . . [his
translation] is the only one I would recommend to a Greekless
reader, and I hope it drives our Rieu, T.E. Lawrence, and Butcher
and Lang.' Peter Levi, *Guardian*

'It gets as close to the veil behind which the real Homer is hidden as
is possible for mortal men.' Bernard Levin, *The Times*

Past Masters

Homer

Jasper Griffin

The *Iliad* and the *Odyssey* stand at the very beginning of Greek literature. Much has been written about their origins and authorship, but Jasper Griffin, although he touches briefly on those questions, is here concerned with the ideas of the poems, which have had such an incalculable influence on the thought and literature of the West. He shows that each of the two epics has its own coherent and suggestive view of the world and of man's place within it.

'Griffin has given us a brilliant and memorable introduction to the two epics.' *Times Literary Supplement*

OPUS

The Philosophy of Aristotle
Second edition

D.J. Allan

In this 'admirably lucid and sympathetic introduction to Aristotle' (*The Times*), the author's purpose is to outline the philosopher's principal doctrines with reference to the circumstances in which they were formed, and to show that it is still worth while to read Aristotle as well as Plato. For the benefit of readers without a classical training, the book opens with a summary of the form of Aristotle's writings and the growth of his philosophy.

OPUS

Ethics since 1900
Third edition

Mary Warnock

For this new edition of her well-established book Mary Warnock
has made a number of additions, in particular a discussion of
Rawls's *A Theory of Justice*. These bring up to date a well-informed
and discriminating account of the main ethical problems which have
been discussed in the present century in England, the United
States and France. A number of writings which deal with these
problems, among them those of Moore, Prichard, Ayer, Stevenson,
Hare and Sartre, have been considered and analysed in some detail.
They have been taken in chronological order and have been selected
from the many books and articles on moral philosophy as those most
likely to be of lasting importance for the subject.

'In this lively and fascinating book Mrs Warnock tells with
admirable clarity the story of the development of English moral
philosophy in the twentieth century . . . most attractively written,
spontaneous, forthright and unfuzzy.' *Times Literary Supplement*

OPUS

Ancient Greek Literature

K.J. Dover and others

K.J. Dover and three other classical scholars have collaborated in
writing this new historical survey of Greek literature from 700 B.C.
to A.D. 550. The book concentrates on the principal authors and
quotes many passages from their work in translation, to allow the
reader to form his own impression of its quality. Attention is drawn
both to the elements in Greek literature and attitudes to life which
are unfamiliar to us, and to the elements which appeal most
powerfully to succeeding generations. Although it is recognised that
this appeal lies above all in the most creative and inventive period
(700–300 B.C.), an account is given of the eight hundred years
which followed, centuries that saw the results of earlier inspirations.
Poetry, tragedy, comedy, history, science, philosophy and oratory
are all examined through the available literature.

Also available in hardback

Oxford Paperbacks

Portrait of Socrates: *The Apology, Crito*, and *Phaedo*

Plato

With an Introduction and Notes by R.W. Livingstone

Livingstone's *Portrait of Socrates* has enjoyed a steady popularity ever since it was first published in 1938. Intended for the ordinary reader who knows no Greek, it contains in an English translation (Jowett's with slight modifications) three works of Plato, the *Apology, Crito* and *Phaedo*, giving a picture of Socrates that no other description could approach. Without guidance a reader of Plato finds some things unintelligible and misses much. This edition contains analyses and discussions of the argument, explanatory notes on the text, and an introduction dealing with the life, times and work of Socrates, and his permanent importance.

'This volume does something that has not been attempted since the eighteenth century, perhaps not since the sixteenth. It presents Greek prose masterpieces in an English dress with an adequate apparatus of introduction and notes.' *Sunday Times*

Oxford Paperbacks

The Fire and the Sun

Iris Murdoch

In this book, based on her 1976 Romanes Lecture, the
distinguished novelist and philosopher discusses Plato's views on art
and examines sympathetically the reasons for his hostility towards
it. She offers a coherent and fully argued account of Plato's theories
of art and of beauty and of their metaphysical background, which
shows also that Plato was aware of the dangers of his own artistry.
The argument more widely concerns the place of art in life, and
includes brief discussion of the ideas of many other thinkers,
including Kant, Tolstoy, Freud and Kierkegaard. The book also
comprises in an accessible form a general view of the development
of Plato's thought.

'Iris Murdoch's book is a triumph of lucid and light-textured
compression as well as of vividly illustrated relevance to our own
world. Her laconic and primly mocking asides are delightful.'
Kathleen Nott, *New Society*

'This little monograph is meant to set out Plato's views rather than
to rebut them. But discreet as it is, Iris Murdoch's counter-attack is
lucid and moving.' George Steiner, *Sunday Times*

A complete list of Oxford Paperbacks, including books in
The World's Classics, Past Masters and OPUS series, can be
obtained from the General Publicity Department, Oxford
University Press, Walton Street, Oxford, OX2 6DP.